What Are the

Theologians Saying NOW?

What Are the

Theologians Saying NOW?

A Retrospective on Several Decades

Monika K. Hellwig

Christian Classics, Inc.

WESTMINSTER, MD

1992

First published, 1992

© 1992 by Monika K. Hellwig

Library of Congress Catalog Card Number: 92-74852

ISBN 0 87061 194 1

Printed in the U.S.A.

This book is dedicated to
Gerard and Virginia Sloyan
in gratitude for their enduring friendship,
wisdom and moral support.

CONTENTS

ACKNOWLEDGEMENTS

Thanks are due in the first place to John McHale, who encouraged and guided the earlier version of this book, written a little over two decades ago, and who once again prompted and encouraged the updated present version.

Recognition is also due to the generosity of Carl C. Landegger for the endowed professorship that made some time available for work on this book, and to my encouraging colleagues in the Theology Department at Georgetown University, who can be counted upon to hail all achievements with enthusiasm.

INTRODUCTION

THE TIME BETWEEN:
A Quarter Century

Change in the Church must usually be reckoned in centuries, so that those of us who are longing for change in some particular matter find movement and development intolerably slow. On the other hand, change since the time of the Second Vatican Council, 1962–65, has been accelerated to a speed at which we not only are bound to be keenly aware of it but are likely to be breathless trying to keep abreast of all that is happening. That in turn has meant that many Catholics who were happy in the Church as they knew it and had grown up in it find themselves deeply distressed, if not actually bitter and angry, or even going so far as to move into schism from the hierarchic Church.

This last reaction is not surprising, given the confusing multitude of voices which ordinary Catholics are hearing. Those of us with the leisure, opportunity and guidance to read extensively, to understand what we read, to see it in the context of the whole history of the Church, and come to some personal discernments of what to take seriously and what to screen out, can be comfortable with a sense of continuity and positive development. But those who do not have these advantages may well see only discontinuity, disunity and chaos. For such readers a synthetic overview of what is being discussed in key issues for today's Church may help to see sense and pattern in what is happening.

It must be noted, however, that this is not nearly as simple a matter now as it was in the immediate aftermath of Vatican II when I wrote *What Are the Theologians Saying?* At that time the key ideas of a handful of European theologians had become official church teaching by their incorporation in the documents of the Council, and had become the foundation for a very radical transformation of the experience and understanding of Church and of redemption. It was easy to identify these theologians and their key ideas, and it was easy to justify the selection because the Council of the whole Church had placed its official stamp of approval on those ideas. While there have been many documents of popes, synods and episcopal conferences since then, many of these have been cautionary rather than ground-breaking, and in any case there has been nothing of the depth and scope of Vatican II.

This leaves a very different kind of task, depending far more on the integrity and wisdom of the synthesizer, on a broader appeal to history and tradition, and on the open-mindedness and good will of the reader. Not only is the task different, but the product is by its nature something more tentative. Not least of the reasons for this is the sheer number of significant published theologians and other scholars who have made and are making significant contributions to unfolding the implications of those key, breakthrough ideas adopted at Vatican II and opening new vistas that stretch far beyond what any of us expected or were prepared for. These contributions come from Scripture scholars, historians, archaeologists, philosophers, canonists, patrologists, moral theologians, systematic theologians, liturgists, sociologists, psychologists and others. In each case, a discovery or development in one field

makes an impact on all the others, and the whole scholarly exchange is constantly in movement.

Many Catholics in our time are inclined to ask
wearily why so much change should be going on all the
time when we were content to have things stay the same
for so long. The answer is that there is a connection
between the two — the long sameness and the rapid
change. What we have to realize is that in these last few
decades the Catholic Church has been assimilating
changes in the world that were held at bay for four hundred years. From the time of the Council of Trent,
1545–1563, to the time of the Second Vatican Council,
1962–1965, much of what was happening in the
modern world was deliberately and systematically
excluded from the life and thought of the Church. For
all those four hundred years Trent was the static reference point for the understanding and practice of the
faith. Though Trent had achieved many good things —
like inventing seminaries to make sure that priests had
all studied theology and had some spiritual formation,
and dealing with abuses, and (through the follow-up
program of Pius V) greatly improving liturgical texts
and practice, and so forth — it had not been able to do
everything, and certainly was not equipped to anticipate

the challenges that would arise in the next four centuries.

The one other council of the Catholic Church in the intervening centuries, the ill-fated First Vatican Council of 1869–1870, fled in panic before an invading army, having barely touched its very limited agenda. In consequence, the agenda for the Second Vatican Council covered all that had arisen since Trent and some matters that had arisen earlier and had not been dealt with. The unresolved questions and challenges were daunting: the questions raised by the sixteenth-century Protestant Reformers concerning the role, interpretation and accessibility of the Scriptures, as well as the accumulated Protestant biblical scholarship, especially from the nineteenth century, which had been forbidden to Catholic students and teachers; the deeper questions involved in the industrial revolution and the changing economic relations among individuals, classes and nations (touched upon by the social encyclicals only from the viewpoint of moral obligations of individuals with economic power); the rise of modern democracy with the different patterns of distribution of power and responsibility involved; developments in the modern natural sciences with profound implications for human self-understanding, human possibilities, and the way people saw the reality of the world about them; modern technology bringing increased communication, greater accumulation of power in the hands of those with access to technology, and whole new fields of moral issues; modern philosophies with emphasis on reason rather than authority, on the human rather than the divine or the cosmos, on individuals rather than communities, on evolutionary rather than static conceptions of reality, on subjectivity rather than claims to be objective, and so forth; the development of the critical historical method, with undeniable evidences that contradicted standard Catholic assumptions about the past; the emergence of the human and social sciences; and much else.

All these things had been happening in human life and thought and, therefore, in the everyday experience of Catholics in the modern world, but official church teaching had generally regarded these modern developments as untrustworthy if not actually manifestations of moral evil. What happened at the Second Vatican Council was something like an earthquake or a volcanic eruption: the pressure had become too great and the questions and problems, as well as the enthusiasms and discoveries, of the modern world burst out of their restraints within the Catholic Church and poured out all over it, changing the landscape. But when something like that happens, one may expect further rumblings and shifts for a very long time, little eruptions of new possibilities and implications here and there, the appearance of new horizons when old landmarks disappear. And this is what we are experiencing now.

CHAPTER ONE

Why and How Do the Church's Teachings Change?

One of the painful issues dividing the Catholic faithful in our day is the question of what can change in the Church's teachings and practice and what must remain the same because it is divinely ordained. Immediately after the Second Vatican Council, many were asking whether change is really possible, because they had come to think of the Church and its teachings as timeless, unaffected by historical circumstances. Now that so much change has occurred and is still constantly taking place, the question has a different focus: Why and how do the Church's teachings change, and by what criteria can we judge what may and what may not change?

Underlying this question is a more fundamental one which functions as a kind of "hidden agenda" in many of the current debates among Catholics. That agenda has to do with the traditional distinction between a divine and a human element in the Church. Many of the conservative Catholics who are troubled by developments like more lay participation, more reliance on individual conscience, less rigid controls, and above all by the kinds of questions which are being raised and debated, are troubled by these developments because of the way they define the divine element in the Church. They may not have reflected on it explicitly, but implicit in their understanding is the unquestioning assumption that the divine element of the Church is in the structures. These are seen as given by God, intrinsic to what Jesus handed over to his earliest followers. Even if some aspects of church organization, sacramental rites and formulations of the teaching are shown to have appeared much later in history, it is assumed that this is only an inevitable unfolding of the original design and intent. It is a design understood to have been made in eternity, therefore having a timeless quality that distinguishes it from all other human events, societies and

ceremonies. Because it comes from eternity and antici-
pates the heavenly resolution of all human lives, the
Church with its hierarchic organization, rituals, rules of
behavior and doctrines of belief is changeless.

An extreme version of this understanding is compli-
cated by a lack of distinction between what is central
and what is peripheral. Such a lack of distinction is the
outcome of a way of appropriating the faith in the first
place, corresponding to the way it was taught. There
has sometimes been a sense that one has a stronger faith
if one does not ask questions or try to understand, but
accepts what is taught simply because it is taught. A
first difficulty with this is that if the teaching is mis-
understood, the misunderstanding will be held just as
firmly as would the true teaching. Because of the lack
of questioning, discussion and debate, it will never be
recognized that there is a misunderstanding. An example of this is a magical understanding of sacramental
efficacy. A second difficulty is that if one does not
question and try to understand the coherence and relationship of beliefs, rules and practices with one another
in a meaningful worldview, the whole structure of the
faith will remain so external to the believer that living by
faith may be reduced to fairly superficial ritual observances not touching the reality of life. An example of

this is the Catholic who attends Mass faithfully, continues to practice sacramental confession, votes against candidates for office who favor legalized abortion, avoids all contraception except natural family planning, but has no hesitation in taking advantage of migrant farm workers, keeping minorities and immigrants out of a residential neighborhood, and realizing the highest profit in business deals without asking at what cost to whom this is being achieved. A third difficulty with the unquestioning appropriation of whatever is taught simply because it is taught is the inability to distinguish between what constitutes the very core of the faith and cannot be removed without destroying the whole, and what is simply transitory, an adaptation to particular times and places, which can well be changed. An example of this failure to distinguish is the way some Catholics continue to insist that only the Tridentine Latin Mass is faithful to the tradition of the Church, not realizing that Latin was first introduced precisely as the vernacular of certain communities of the Western Roman Empire in the third century, and that the Tridentine canon was selected and adapted from a great plurality of forms under Pius V in the late sixteenth century in order to correct abuses which are no longer a problem in our time.

Some of the criteria for distinguishing the relative importance of various doctrines, structures and rules will be discussed in Chapter 2. But the basis for those criteria is in the prior question about the divine and human elements in the Church. Can we really assume that the structures that have been handed down to us are the divine element of the Church? The answer of many contemporary theologians who deal with the theology of Church in particular is that this identification is simplistic and puts the emphasis in the wrong place. Basing themselves both on the tradition as brought to focus in *Lumen gentium* (Vatican II's Dogmatic Constitution on the Church) and on the known history of the structures, these theologians define the nature of the Church in terms of its goal and mission. Thus Hans Küng, in *The Structures of the Church,* had already pointed to the theological significance of what we now know of the actual history of particular structures. Eugene Hillman, in a series of writings beginning with *The Church as Mission* (in which he set out his foundational theme), traces the relationship between visible representation mediated by rituals, organizational forms, etc., and the redemptive movement in the world and its history and peoples for the sake of which the visible representation exists.

In *Church: The Human Story of God,* the third volume of his important trilogy on the significance of Jesus in human history, Edward Schillebeeckx has shown that, far from being divinely guaranteed in patterns drawn from the past, the structures of the Church are to be judged by the promises of God's reign among us which calls for constant conversion and change. Avery Dulles, in a number of recent writings, such as *The Reshaping of Catholicism* and *The Catholicity of the Church,* while always concerned with the visible and actual reality of the Church, and while always linking his reflections to the official statements of the self-understanding of the Church, also insists that what specifies the Catholic Church is not primarily the containing structure but what it contains — namely, the inner vision and style by which the community tries to be fully and authentically Christian.

Many other voices might be added to these as part of a groundswell of those seeing the Church as movement, as people of God on pilgrimage in history. Notable among these are many of those who style themselves liberation theologians, such as Juan Luis Segundo in *Theology for Artisans of a New Humanity,* and the recent martyr, Ignacio Ellacuria, in *Freedom Made Flesh.* But the question must be raised explicitly:

if the structures are not the divine element of the Church, what is? The answer to this is simple, though not offering the same easy black and white criteria for orthodoxy. The divine element of the Church is Jesus as its source and inspiration, the Holy Spirit as its continuing dynamic life force, and the transcendent God who calls it to strive towards the fulness of the divine reign in human history. But if this is what we mean by the divine element, then the human element consists of every kind of human cooperation, adequate or inadequate, appropriate or inappropriate, graced or sinful. The structures of the Church are always the outcome of the divine inspiration as understood and implemented humanly, and therefore fallibly, and as grasped in a particular historical context with the prejudices of particular language, class, cultural and political biases. And this means that these structures must constantly remain under scrutiny.

If we take this understanding of what is divine and what is human in the Church seriously, the question of what can change in the teachings of the Church, and how and why, becomes not only a central and pressing question but also one that requires continual discernment in the Spirit. It is not susceptible to easy, prepackaged answers. Moreover, it raises sensitive and subtle questions about the role of the local Church, and particularly about the role of the laity in the continuing process of discernment — questions that will be touched on in Chapter 3.

As all changes that come about are not necessarily good, we are still confronted in our times with the question that John Henry Cardinal Newman considered in his book *An Essay on the Development of Christian Doctrine*: what constitutes development faithful to the tradition, and what constitutes a break from the tradition? This book of Newman's has been very influential among twentieth-century theologians because it is based on history, and history is our principal resource in understanding human problems. However, what has been helpful in the book has not been the detailed way that Newman worked out his criteria (which are actually rather elusive and difficult to apply to contemporary questions) but the general idea of the book: namely, that if we study the development of doctrine in the past, we gain a good sense of how the Church comes to certitude and to authoritative statements. It is reasonable to suppose that this process continues throughout history and, therefore, in our own times. It is quite clear that the development did not stop with the great councils of antiquity (before the schism between East and West), nor with the Fourth Lateran Council in 1215, which seemed so decisive, nor with the Council of Constance of 1414–18, which resolved the schism of rival claimants to the papacy, declaring that a council of the Church had higher authority than the pope. While virtually all Catholics would agree with the statement of continuing development thus far, many conservative Catholics of our time have difficulty accepting the idea that the same principle applies to the Council of Trent of 1545–63.

This is an issue which, whether implicitly or explicitly, is causing tension and divisions in many places in the Church. It is important to understand what is at stake. The majority of post–Vatican II Catholics are happy with the changes that have taken place, allowing more freedom and initiative to lay people, offering more life and intelligibility in public worship, more friendly relations with other Christians and people of other religions. To most of us this seems sheer gain, and most do not ask by what right or authority changes are introduced. However, it is important to understand (even though not agreeing with) the logic of anti–Vatican II conservatism. Those who hold this position see the Council of Trent as different both from the ancient councils of the relatively undivided Church, and from the medieval councils of the Western Church. These could all be part of a continuing process of development. What is seen as different about the Council of Trent is that it defined in great detail (and claiming definitive authority) what constitutes Catholic faith and practice as distinguished from Protestant communities and their teachings. Moreover, the teachings of Trent were incorporated in the official standard curricula and textbooks of the newly founded seminaries (at a time when lay people simply did not study theology), and were passed on in an ahistorical way, more or less unchanged for four hundred years. There was, of course, a council during that time, the First Vatican Council of 1869–70, but this was seen as reinforcing the teachings of Trent and indeed emphasizing even more strongly the distinction between Catholic and Protestant. The combination of the long period without change (as described already in the Introduction) and the method of exposition, which was ahistorical (and reflected from the seminary textbooks into the popular instructional catechisms), produced a very strong impression of changelessness. Indeed it became a frequently heard boast that, while Protestant communions might change with the times and assimilate modern secular ideas, the Catholic

Church was changeless, an impregnable fortress amid the contingencies of history.

Given this experience, it is little to be wondered at that there should be considerable numbers of Catholics today who cling to convictions shaped out of that experience, and who find a theoretical explanation to justify their stance. One common version of this is the thesis that Trent definitively established the doctrinal and disciplinary and ritual prescriptions which define Catholicism in perpetuity, while Vatican II was a pastoral council with no dogmatic authority. Something similar is said of the social encyclicals of the popes of the past century or so: they are exhortatory documents whose reflections on social justice and peace do not touch the significant core of the faith.

No one should ridicule this position, because it has a strong logic based on recent experience. What it lacks, however, is historical depth. A knowledge of the early development of the Christian liturgy, of the writings of the first six hundred years, of the debates that went into the making of the church councils throughout the centuries, of the shaping of medieval philosophy and theology, of the ever-changing relationship between spirituality and theology, and other historical factors, presents the same issues in a very different perspective, in which continuing development and change may be taken for granted, and the real question is why and how the church teaching changes. This is the real question because, in answering it, we are in a better position to see the continuity and to judge where it lies amid the plurality of voices in our own time.

The great theologian Karl Rahner, who died in 1984, and whose influence has been pervasive both in the Second Vatican Council and in subsequent theological work, suggests an authoritative starting point for this effort to understand the how and the why of doctrinal change. In the essay "The Development of Dogma" in *Theological Investigations* Vol. I, Rahner points out the special, guaranteed authority of what we read in Scripture. Therefore the development of doctrine that can be traced in the New Testament itself provides an approved model. One characteristic that is evident in the New Testament lines of doctrinal development is that they show more than a logical unfolding of what was already implicit; they show a development that is based on the continuing reflection and changing experience of the young community of believers.

The question arises, of course, whether this is something that is appropriate only to the beginning, as the foundations of the Church and of patterns of

Christian life and belief were being laid. If we were to think of the Church as static and defined by the past, we might conclude that what was required to set up the Church in the first place might be quite different from what is required to maintain it in its timeless sameness. However, if we define the Church in terms of its goal and purpose, the welcoming of the reign of God among all peoples and all human situations, then we might well suppose that the way people struggled to understand their role and calling in the first fervor is the way later generations would also struggle to understand and respond to their calling. In other words, the question looks very different from the perspective of each of these two ways of understanding the Church and the purpose of its existence.

A very good example of this in New Testament times and our own times is that of "inculturation" — that is, of adaptation to cultural differences of various peoples. Very early the question arose about Jewish food laws and other observances of ritual cleanliness. Jesus himself had observed these laws and so had his disciples, though giving priority to human need on suitable occasions, in the best Jewish tradition. Could it be right to dispense with these for gentile believers, and (even more daringly) could it be right for Jewish followers of the way of Jesus to abandon some of these observances in order to join wholeheartedly with gentile members of the community at Eucharist and its accompanying fellowship meal?

Similar questions have arisen in our times. Can time-honored customs and observances, like the compulsory Lenten fast, or kneeling during the Canon of the Mass, or Latin as the language of the liturgy, be dispensed with in adapting to the contemporary culture of the West? Can ethnic variations in liturgical celebration be tolerated, or will they destroy the unity of the Church? The reply according to Rahner's suggestion, is that if this is the kind of development we see in the New Testament, then we have a good precedent for continuing to make such adaptations when they truly serve the reconciliation of the human community to God's reign among us. But this answers only one half of the question. The indispensable second half is: who shall decide, or discern, whether a particular change or adaptation serves human reconciliation with God and with God's reign in all human affairs? It is clear that this cannot be a simple matter of hierarchic authority declaring an answer. From the nature of the case, both the question and the possible answers come from the experience of the whole community of the faithful, and the discernment does not begin with the voice of authority but with the voice of experience. The question, therefore, of who decides or discerns resolves itself into a question about the pattern of exchange through which the discernment takes place.

This is why one of the most debated and discussed issues in Catholic theology today is the question of "reception." Posed in 1972 by Yves Congar in the article "Reception as an Ecclesiological Reality" in *Election and Consensus in the Church* (*Concilium* 77), the topic has since been widely discussed. Among the many authors now writing on the subject, perhaps the most creative and significant is Luis Bermejo in *Infallibility on Trial* (Westminster, Md.: Christian Classics, Inc., 1992). The word *reception* refers to the assimilation of beliefs, rules of conduct, observances, and so forth, into the life and understanding of the community. The reason for the emergence of reception as a central idea in the discussion of change and development in the Church has to do with contemporary Catholic experience of the way the Church functions. In the experience of contemporary Catholics, mandates and instructions come out from Rome as though from their place of origin. Seldom do the communities of the faithful have any sense that they themselves are participants in the discernment process. Therefore the question of reception focuses on assimilation by the local Church of edicts issued from a higher authority, and often enough it focuses on the extreme tension created by lack of attention by authority to the context and experience of the local community. However, the issue begins with the perception of what has been happening in the local Churches over the centuries, and how worldwide unity has been built.

This is a topic on which contemporary theology continues to return to Cardinal Newman's essay *On Consulting the Faithful in Matters of Doctrine*. The implication of Newman's historical study is that consulting the received or accepted piety and belief of the faithful is prior to any hierarchic teaching. In an explicit way this has been practiced in our own time in some instances, such as the definition of the assumption of Mary as dogma in 1950, and in recent pastoral letters of the American bishops on peace and on a just economy. This process as the norm was described by Bernard Lonergan, longtime professor at the Gregorian University, who also died in 1984, in his *Tractatus de Trinitate*. He explains that in the formation of church teaching in the past what we see is, not primarily a downward movement from the hierarchic authority to the experts and from there to the people, but an upward movement based on the living faith experience of the people. That living faith experience finds expression first in concrete patterns of life-style, worship and belief, is then theoretically formulated by various professional experts, and is finally sifted and synthesized into official teaching.

The pattern of this as observed from the early centuries of the Church's history is very helpful in appreciating what is happening in our own time. Lonergan suggests a kind of spiraling pattern. The experience of the community in changing cultures, economies and other circumstances prompts new questions. These may refer to entirely new matters, they may be a new way of looking at established teachings and practices, or they may arise from the unintelligibility of old formulations or the inapplicability of old rules. When that happens, as it must constantly, people turn to various kinds of experts — theologians, historians, biblical scholars, canonists, philosophers and so forth. The matter is discussed in a more systematic way, in terms of the coherence of the faith as a whole, in terms of the original context and purpose of the teaching or practice, and in terms of the contemporary context for the question or problem that has been raised. In most cases (as, for instance, in the medieval discussion of grace and sacraments), the matter is resolved in this discussion and quietly becomes the official teaching in course of time. This has been called the ordinary magisterium. Only in a few cases does it happen that spectacular disagreements occur which disturb people sufficiently that they appeal to hierarchic authority to settle the matter by a solemn statement, as happened in the ecumenical councils of the ancient Church. Such solemn statements or definitions have been called the extraordinary magisterium.

Several points must be noted in relation to this process. First of all, it is not a tidy way of resolving any questions once and for all. It is more like a spiraling movement. The questions that arise from today's world and experience will reach the experts tomorrow. When the moral theologians or the systematic theologians understand the dimensions of the question, they will want to turn to the work of biblical scholars to find out what resources Scripture may offer for the solution, and to patrologists for resources in the early history of the Church, as well as to historians, canonists and other experts. All of this takes time. If the solutions proposed converge, it will still take time for them to gain the status of church teachings. If they do not converge and authority must intervene explicitly, that will certainly take much longer again. The result of such inevitable delays is that official teaching is often addressing past problems and questions, while new questions are those which really concern the faithful of the time. Continued development and change is what we must expect.

The second point to be noted about this is that it throws a different light on what has been called "dissent." If church teaching and practice were really static, as appeared in the centuries after the Council of Trent, then the question of dissent is hardly a question: the dissenter is simply wrong. But if church teaching is in a continual process of development and adaptation to new circumstances and demands, and if that process comes from the experience and spontaneous response of the faithful, through the systematic and scholarly reflection of the experts to the hierarchic authority of the Church, dissent is an integral factor in the shaping of church tradition. It must be heard and studied attentively and respectfully, as well as prayerfully.

A third point to be noted concerning this spiraling process is how much it depends on discernment which is both well informed and very sensitive to the Spirit breathing in the Church. A remarkable saying of John XXIII, when asked to make a heavy-handed statement of the official teaching in a certain matter, was: "I am not here to *tell* the Church what the Spirit says, but to observe attentively and see *in* the Church what the Spirit is saying." It was this attitude and this understanding of his office which led him with such dogged determination against all opposition to call a general council of all the local Churches in which needs, difficulties and questions from the local Churches could be brought to the reflection of the universal Churches. Although the deliberations in council were made by the bishops, a vital role in this was played by the *periti,* the various types of experts who advised their bishops. These people were drawing in part on their professional expertise, but also in large measure on their knowledge of the experience and circumstances of the faithful in the local Churches. All of this was, and always is, relevant to the Church's discernment of what serves the reign of God in human society.

A final point to note is that this understanding of the process shaping church tradition takes very seriously the experience of ordinary Christians in their particular contexts. This does not mean that church tradition must adapt to what people would like, but rather that it must adapt to what they learn from experience about the demands and possibilities of the redemption of all facets of human history. In practice the distinction between what church members like or find more convenient on the one hand, and what they learn of the workings of the redemption in their own lives and societies on the other hand, may be a very difficult one to make. But we are not living in a pre-programmed society. We are living among human beings, all of whom have free will and are in some measure unpredictable, so that constant adjustment in response to the decisions of others is one of the tasks inherent in human existence. Moreover, we are not living in the pristine world of God's good creating, but in a world marred and distorted in many ways through the consequences of destructive human choices. And we have been graced with the divine Spirit and enlisted in the work of transformation which is the redemption. All of us, therefore, are called to live by the Spirit, which is a spirit of prophecy — that is, of critical evaluation.

A remarkable demonstration of what this can mean in practice was given in a short but significant article by Walter Principe, a theologian at St. Michael's, Toronto, whose primary expertise is in medieval theology, but who has also taken a great interest in contemporary developments and has served on the International Theological Commission for the Universal Church. His article "When 'Authentic' Teachings Change" in *The Ecumenist* of July-August, 1987, lists specific examples of changes, showing how continued popular and scholarly discussion had prompted them. Examples given are: authoritative church legitimation of slavery, which quietly faded into the background and was at last explicitly repudiated by Vatican II; official endorsement of torture of prisoners was reversed in 1816; the teaching on religious liberty for which John Courtney Murray was reprimanded and silenced became the official position of the Church at Vatican II; Pius XII rejected the teaching previously understood to be in the ordinary magisterium of the Church, that outside the Catholic Church there could be no salvation; Vatican II went further and changed the teaching of Pius XII himself that the Mystical Body of Christ was identical with the Roman Catholic Church; several decrees of the Pontifical Biblical Commission (which scholars and teachers were expected to observe) were actually changed in the course of the twentieth century in response to further scholarship; the commitment to a monogenist understanding of human origins, taught authoritatively by Pope Pius XII in *Humani generis* in 1950, has quietly been dropped; termination of ectopic pregnancies, once considered sinful abortion, is no longer questioned; considerable changes took place in the course of history in the theology and practice of the sacraments as officially taught; and so forth.

What all of this amounts to is that the certainty which we have in the faith is not of a kind that lifts us out of the struggle of human interaction in history. It does not relieve us of the need to use our intelligence and critical faculty, or of the risk of making mistakes. Nor does it excuse us from the general human challenge of reconciling the personal quest for truth and a good life with the need for community harmony. The existence of strong centralized authority in the Catholic Church does not take away adult responsibilities from Catholic believers.

However, this understanding leaves some urgent questions, not least of which is: What is it, in a constantly shifting context, that is central and enduring in our faith? And this is the topic of the following chapter.

Suggestions for Further Reading

All the books mentioned in this chapter are informative and help the reader to understand what is at stake in the issues discussed here. However, some assume more background knowledge than the general reader is likely to have.

Anyone who has not already read Hans Küng's *The Structures of the Church* (Notre Dame: University of Notre Dame Press; London: Sheed & Ward, 1968) will probably appreciate the clarity of style in which it offers the history and theological background of the questions of development in church teaching. Though intensely critical and primarily concerned with the ecumenical aspects of change, *The Church Is Different* by Robert Adolfs (New York: Harper & Row; London: Burns & Oates, 1966) is very helpful in gaining a historical perspective.

Three collections of essays may also be helpful to the non-specialist. *The Teaching Authority of the Believers,* edited by J. B. Metz and Edward Schillebeeckx (Edinburgh: T. & T. Clark, Ltd., 1985), gives brief summaries of significant contributions to the question of community participation. *Concilium* 67: *History, the Self-Understanding of the Church* (New York: Herder & Herder, 1971) describes how this participation functions in practice. *That They Might Live,* edited by Michael Downey (New York: Crossroad Publishing Co., 1991), offers helpful positive perspectives on possibilities of lay participation for the future.

CHAPTER TWO

What Is Central and Enduring in Our Faith?

As shown in Chapter 1, there is constant change and development in the faith and teaching of the Church, because it is made up of living, creative, interacting people in a constantly changing world. This demands further reflection on what then constitutes the continuity and oneness of the Church. All generations have had to ask this question explicitly or implicitly, but in their answers there has not always been the same emphasis. For instance, "apostolic succession," which in recent times has focused on the claim to an unbroken chain of priestly ordinations and episcopal consecrations going back to the original disciples of Jesus (an increasingly problematic claim in the light of historical evidence), originally meant something different. In the writers of the earliest Christian centuries, apostolic succession focused on the reliability of the bishops' teaching because that teaching could be seen to be in accord with that of the apostolic Church of the very beginning.

In the early Christian centuries, the formulation of what was central and enduring came to be summarized for adult newcomers to the faith in the form of pre-baptismal creeds. The formula known to us as the Apostles' Creed (though it cannot actually be traced back to them as a formula then in use) is typical of the early creeds. How much community participation and reflection went into the making of these has been shown by Catholic University of America theologian Berard Marthaler in *The Creed* (Mystic, Conn.: Twenty-Third Publications, 1987). It is clear that the words of the creeds were not revealed by the transcendent God as words, nor even spoken by Jesus as words. Yet these particular words are at the heart of what is central and enduring in the Church. They represent the community's prayerful reflection on their experience of Jesus and his impact in human history, on what they learned by living as disciples of Jesus, and on how they came to see the divine in that process.

The question, therefore, of what is enduring and central in the Church is related to the question of the content of revelation, and yet it is not exactly the same question. Much theological literature in our times has been concerned with the delicate question of understanding the inseparable reciprocity of God's self-revelation and the human reception of that revelation in the language, culture and imagery of the recipients. Already in the early 1960s, Edward Schillebeeckx was concerned with a disentangling of terms we use and claims we make in theology concerning revelation. His two volumes on the subject were issued in English translation under the title *Revelation and Theology* (Kansas City: Sheed & Ward, 1967, 1968). Leading American Catholic theologian Avery Dulles explored the same issue and its ecumenical implications in his book *Revelation and the Quest for Unity* (Washington: Corpus Books, 1968), in which he followed through the logical consequences of Vatican II's Constitution on Divine Revelation, *Dei Verbum* of 1965. And in the following year, to facilitate the discussion, he set out the entire historical context for this in *Revelation Theology* (New York: Herder & Herder, 1969). A later development in this discussion of the appropriate ways to understand the divine-human cooperation involved in revelation has emerged in the work of the liberation theologians of Latin America. Gustavo Gutierrez, Juan Luis Segundo, Jon Sobrino and others have raised the question of continuing cooperation in God's self-revelation in present-day history, more particularly on the part of the poor and disregarded populations of the contemporary world.

What emerges out of all this discussion is that there is no way we can reach the pure revelation of God separated from all human interpretation. God speaks to us in creation, in our own conscience and consciousness, in our individual human experiences, in our relationships, our societies, our history. The self-revelation of God and of the divine purposes in creation is speech only in an analogous sense, and therefore does not come to us in formulated propositions or specific images and symbols. It is mediated into these by human attempts to express and pass on what has been learned at a deeper level. Although the propositional formulae of the faith are important, they never capture the whole reality nor capture it in the one and only way in which it might be expressed.

This has proved very important in ecumenical encounters. Many issues which, after Trent, divided Catholic and Protestant — as it seemed, forever — have turned out to be more tractable in the light of the Vatican II documents. One reason for this is that our interpretation of classic texts (such as the Scriptures and the early creeds) is always both problematic and to some degree autobiographical. The meanings and connotations of words, phrases and propositional statements cannot be objectively fixed anywhere, but are always dependent on recognition in those who receive them; and that recognition is always dependent on the particular experiences of those recipients, including the language and usages they have been taught, the social structures and relationships they have known, the types of arguments they have been trained to expect and respect, and much else. This alone should, and in the contemporary world does, lead us to be more humble about the nature of our own access to the truth, and more open to the possibility that other approaches or interpretations also give access to the truth.

What holds true in a general way about all interpretation is intensified when we are dealing with attempts to formulate our relationship with the transcendent God, and the ultimate meaning of human lives and the history of the human race, as well as the situation of that race in creation. Words, concepts, images and more complex symbols and abstractions are all quite incapable of really grasping reality on this scale. The best we can do is to glimpse, attempt analogies, catch partial insights and meanings. In this context especially, the kinds of claims to final and unchangeable certitude about the truth of verbal formulations (which were not uncommonly made in the past for Catholic doctrinal statements) need to become more cognizant of the nature of our access to the mystery of the transcendent God.

If this seems to make the very idea of revelation elusive and problematic, then it will help to understand why theologians continue to be preoccupied with revelation, in spite of the more traditional thesis that revelation was complete with the death of the last apostle who had known Jesus in the flesh, and that this complete revelation has been passed on to us in the Church. Contemporary theologians think that it is not at all evident what is meant by the word *revelation* as used in Christian faith. We have always realized that, in the last analysis, what is "unveiled" or shown is God in relationship to the human community and to each human individual — God as source, savior and meaning, God as powerful and merciful, gracious and generous, providing fulfillment and challenge, making life worthwhile and purposeful. Obviously, this is something that must unfold in the experience of each believer; it is not enough to pass it along in a verbal report. And yet, after earliest infancy, our experience is never simply raw or primitive, uninterpreted, unshaped by others. Expression and interpretation draw on experience, but experience is shaped by what we are taught to look for and to expect. Any account of our own experience is always shaped by the language and symbol systems and other aspects of culture which we have been taught.

This shows that, while the words cannot wholly capture the revelation, we cannot dispense with them either. They become a vital part of what is central and permanent. This applies in the first place to Scripture. The Church in Vatican II, taking modern scholarship into account, does not claim that all the Bible is revelation nor that all revelation is in the Bible. It claims that the Bible offers us the classic instance from which we can understand how and what God reveals. However, even the Bible is not to be read woodenly, as though the distance in time, language and culture poses no problems of interpretation. For insight into the way the Bible offers the classic instance of revelation which guides us in our own receptivity to the divine, the work of René Latourelle, of the Gregorian University in Rome, continues to be extremely helpful. His book *Theology of Revelation* points out three key aspects of the biblical

understanding of revelation. First of all, there is a progressive understanding of revelation. The self-revealing
God becomes more personal and specific in the
demands of faith and conversion of life. From the
Christian perspective of the New Testament, these
demands find their final and concrete definition in the
person of Jesus, who speaks clear words in human language, and gives ordinary human signs of love and
trust and challenge. If Scripture is the classic instance,
offering the model, then it follows that it is the nature of
revelation in all our lives to be progressive. We may
expect it to consist of signs that become gradually
clearer and of demands that become more specific and
far-reaching. This should be so not only for each individual but for all of us together — the community of
believers, and the community of the human race.

Secondly, as Father Latourelle points out, Scripture
speaks mainly of God as self-revealing in the history of
the chosen people, but it also refers back to the word of
God already spoken in creation. In other words, what is
clarified and brought to focus in the special events nar-
rated in the Bible is continuous with the rest of experience, and interprets the whole of human experience and
human existence.

Perhaps, however, the third point in Latourelle's discussion is the most significant. The events of history do not, by themselves, constitute revelation, nor does the simple narration of these events constitute revelation. It is by prophetic interpretation that they become revelatory. The prophet is one who speaks for God, telling the meaning of events happening in the world. Therefore the same events can either become revelatory or fail to do so. Roman or Syrian records of the Maccabean wars, for instance, would not offer us the testimony of the self-revealing God which we have in the Jewish account.

Any reference to prophecy and prophets raises, of course, the further question of how people can be speaking for God, how they know what to say, and how particular words or expressions can become canonical or binding for a whole tradition. While the recognition of prophecy and its distinctions from false claims is a broad topic, for Christians it has a precise focus: namely, the person of Jesus. Revelation is a continuing dialogue between God and the human community, but the center of the conversation is Jesus Christ. As has long been recognized in Christian tradition, Jesus does not simply bring the word of revelation, but is that word in his person. He is the event as well as the interpreter of the event — a human individual totally open to all the possibilities of being and of love held out by God. As a prophetic interpretation, he explains the nature of God as a huge welcome to the existence and becoming of all men.

When we take the humanity of Jesus seriously, it emerges that he is first and foremost the recipient of the revelation of the transcendent God whom he calls "Father" in such a way that he is able to share his experience with us and reflect to us the face of the Father. The Gospels of the New Testament are more insistent on the full humanity of Jesus than Christians have often been since then. They show Jesus constantly praying to the Father, growing in wisdom, admitting that there were things that he did not know, and gradually becoming more fully aware of his own mission and destiny. The whole New Testament shows Jesus gradually becoming more fully aware of the meaning of all human existence within a good creation and within a history that had and has suffered distortion by destructive deeds and their consequences. He is, therefore, a revelation of what it means to be truly human, and through this he becomes the revelation of the divine.

It is true, of course, that our faith asserts that Jesus is Lord, uniquely Son of God, and the clear and definitive Word of God spoken in history. But this makes sense only if we realize that it is a fully human word that is spoken. When he interpreted his own mission, Jesus struggled to express in Aramaic words, drawn from his culture and from his personal and social environment, his human understanding of the divine meaning of his own existence and life in the world. He also struggled to express that meaning in typically Jewish gestures and signs, and in the way he shaped his own life and responded to others who shaped it.

All of this is consequential for our understanding of the process of revelation and of our own role in that process. When the Apostles pass on the message of Jesus in their sermons, they do not begin by passing on what he said. We know from the early chapters of the Acts of the Apostles that they first speak of their own Easter experience, their participation in the resurrection event. They testify, not at second hand, but out of their own participation in the event. The revelation they saw in Jesus was first and foremost his way of meeting death and his way of bursting the bonds of death. They were inviting others into that experience. The content of revelation, the meaning of Jesus, was something that could not be entirely communicated in words. What the apostolic community received from Jesus was primarily the full human experience of his presence, his companionship, his friendship, lending meaning and purpose to their lives. Only secondarily and in the context of this friendship did they receive explanatory words. They received the revelation by living in his company and following in his way, and out of their reflection on this experience they gave utterance in their own words to a further prophetic interpretation, extending the presence of Christ in the world by their own presence.

It is this model that indicates the nature of our own role in the process, and gives a key to the search for what is central and enduring in our faith. It is first of all a way of life, inspired by a shared vision of reality and its possibilities, and supported experientially by a well-grounded hope. Consequently, what must be central and enduring is, in the first place, a continuing life of discipleship in the community, trying to share the vision and hope of Jesus, and living by it in changing circumstances. And that in turn means continuing active reflection, discernment and critical evaluation by all believers. Because circumstances vary and situations change, discipleship of Jesus requires more than following a set of explicit and detailed instructions. It involves willingness to learn from one's own contemporary experience, and to grow into progressively deeper understanding of the meaning and demands of the gospel.

That kind of continuity is ensured less by passing on verbal formulations and more by drawing succeeding generations and newcomers into the community that truly lives such a life. Yet we all know that words play some role in this — the words of the liturgy, of Scripture, of hymnody and devotions, of the tales of heroic deeds and holy lives, and also the words of systematic explanation, of exhortation and prescription, and so forth. From the beginning we have some formulations that are given a special place in the tradition: the apostolic community gave us a classic collection in the New Testament, but we also have the creeds and some very venerable liturgical and catechetical texts which have come to play a central role in the tradition.

An important question arises about texts formulated after the apostolic age. Are they less sacred, less important, less fixed for future times? Certainly the words of the apostolic community are unique because of the closeness of their authors to the historical Jesus. Those who walked in his company had an experience definitive for all time, and are witnesses in a way no one else can be. But this testimony would have little significance for us if it were only the account of a past event. What

makes it significant is that it guides our interpretation of
the same revelation in which we are participants. Out of
the living experience of the shared life of the community
in different times and circumstances, successive generations gave their own interpretations in words. In the
course of time the verbal formulations changed quite a
lot.

One might be tempted to ask at what point revelation
ends and ordinary theology, liturgy and catechetics
begin. But the question would be as meaningless as
asking "Where do the woods end and the trees begin?"
All this is participation in the continuing unfolding of
revelation, not simply a recording of what was revealed
before, played over and over again. Because revelation
is personal communion of people with God, it cannot
be played over like an old recording.

This, however, is not the whole answer to the practical question. If all participation in the life of faith and
discipleship is participation in revelation, does it mean
that every word or explanation is just as good as any
other, or is there a hierarchy and a principle of discrimi-
nation? How can we know that people who give
expression to their experience and understanding are not
fooling themselves? And what becomes of the Catholic
Church's claims for its dogmatic teachings, its sacra-

mental power, and its authoritative guidelines on moral issues? Words are a community product and a community property. When the Christian community wants to share its experience, it has to agree on the way it explains itself. It has to find agreement on its common understanding of the world, the community, its history and its destiny, and most of all on its understanding of God. It needs a common language for this. It needs a common statement of its prophetic interpretation of the events in which God is self-revealed in the community — the events of the life of Jesus and of the original formation of the Church. Moreover, it needs reference points or frames of reference for the interpretation of divine self-revelation in our time. Sacramental celebration, doctrinal formulations, and moral guidelines provide such needed reference points.

In this process it is inevitable that the earliest texts and structures will need to be the most stable because they are, so to speak, the foundation on which the unity and community of the Churches is built. More recent, more local or particular determinations, and those which concern more peripheral issues, are therefore also more readily changeable. In this, authority is a necessary mediator whose role is to be attentive to the living dialogue with the divine in the community, to encourage prophecy, and to harmonize creative initiatives and responses. Continuity and unity would serve no purpose if they were simply an empty shell. Revelation is truly happening when people creatively participate in the encounter. This means that new events happen, new words are spoken and new visions are projected.

This in turn means that the unexpected, the unprecedented is integral to the history of the redemption of the world. What is central and enduring in the faith is, not a collection of ready-formulated eternal and unchanging truths, but the undying fidelity of God reflected in a persevering struggle for fidelity in the community of the faithful.

Suggestions for Further Reading

Here, as at the end of the first chapter, it must be admitted that the significant works on revelation and on the creeds mentioned in the chapter may prove difficult for the non-specialist, at least without further introduction.

It is for this reason that I wrote two small earlier books, now out of print, which may still prove helpful to those who can find them: *Tradition: The Catholic Story Today* (Dayton, Ohio: Pflaum Press, 1974) and *The Christian Creeds: A Faith to Live By* (Dayton, Ohio: Pflaum Press, 1973). I have tried to do something similar in *Understanding Catholicism* (New York: Paulist Press, 1981).

Those who are willing to give it close attention will appreciate an older book of Yves Congar, *The Meaning of Tradition* (New York: Hawthorn Books; London: Burns & Oates, 1964) now available only in libraries. Similarly, such readers will find *The Survival of Dogma* by Avery Dulles (New York: Doubleday & Co., 1971) both enlightening and satisfying.

CHAPTER THREE

What Authority Does the Local Church Have?

Most intelligent Catholic layfolk might not identify the question about the authority of the local Church as an urgent one for our times. They would probably point to practical issues such as the status of the divorced and remarried, the question of contraception, the right of pastors to withhold the baptism of children unless their parents come to pre-baptismal instructions, the status of teenagers who have stopped going to church on Sundays, the continuing requirement of celibacy for clergy in an increasingly priestless Church, the exclusion of women from decision-making and from the more respected ministries in the Church, and finally, perhaps, the extent and justification of papal authority.

It may seem strange to interested and widely read adult Catholics of our time that so much theology is being published on topics that seem of much less immediate concern. The reason for this apparent distancing from the issues is that, underlying the obvious issues, is a hidden agenda that blocks the solution of those issues at every turn. The hidden agenda is not a matter of something that someone is trying to hide or is even aware of hiding. The term refers to the way a discussion can be deadlocked when both (or all) sides presume they are making the same basic assumptions as a starting point when in fact they are not. In all the issues listed above, those involved suffer intense frustration because different parties to the debate are making quite different assumptions about authority in the Church but seem generally to be unaware of this fact.

In modern times the question of authority in the Catholic Church has often been reduced to the discussion of papal infallibility, which is much too narrow a focus. It is not surprising, however, that this issue should be in the forefront, because it was defined explicitly only at the First Vatican Council in 1870, because it was bitterly disputed within the Church at the same time, and because it sharpened considerably the contrast between Catholic and Protestant ways of understanding the Church and its task. Even if the focus is not as narrow as the infallibility claim (which has, after all, been specifically invoked only on two occasions), attention is generally turned to the pope in person and to regulations, exhortations and declarations assumed to come from him personally. Many Catholics have an uneasy feeling that unless the role of the pope has been dealt with in relation to development of doctrine, revelation and continuity in the Church, the issues have been evaded. For this reason, the question will still be dealt with in this chapter, but as part of the larger question: What is the basis for authority in the Church, and what therefore should be the role of the local Church?

For some decades, theologians have been concerned with the history of the structures which the Church has today. Already in the mid-twentieth century, for instance, Dominican theologian Yves Congar, in the book entitled *Tradition and Traditions,* demonstrated that there has always been much more variety and change in structures of authority in the Church than most Catholics — including clergy, canonists and theologians, and officials of the Holy See — realized.

Because they assumed a static and unified church organization, it was also easy to assume that the pattern was set by Christ and should never be changed. But when we study history with an open mind and a critical eye, we come to realize that the authority structures we know arose in stages and in response to particular historical circumstances, and (it must be said) often as the outcome of a power struggle that was not demonstrably pure in intention. This leads to further questions about the desirability, in view of the gospel, of certain ways of exercising authority, certain claims about the binding force of pronouncements, attempts to silence discussion and objections, and so forth.

The earlier work of Hans Küng, beginning with *Council, Reform and Reunion* (New York: Sheed & Ward, 1961, written after the announcement by Pope John XXIII that he would call a council) and continuing with *The Structures of the Church* (New York: Thomas Nelson & Sons, 1964) and *The Church* (New York: Doubleday & Co., 1967), began to draw some conclusions from the historical findings. At that time his conclusions appeared very bold and were sharply disputed. In the intervening decades, however, many further studies by careful and balanced thinkers have followed in the same direction. In *Council over Pope?* (New

York: Herder & Herder, 1969), Francis Oakley, professor at Williams College, presented a detailed evaluation of the medieval sources of today's Catholic ecclesiology. He showed from the medieval councils of the Western Church, from the discussion in the university theological faculties of the time, and from secular and ecclesial political moves, the strength of the conciliarist argument. This argument defends the position that has never been questioned in the Eastern Churches — namely, that the authority exercised by human persons in the Church is essentially collegial, resting upon community discernment in the Spirit. In 1983, in the book *Magisterium: Teaching Authority in the Catholic Church,* Jesuit theologian Francis Sullivan, professor at the Gregorian University in Rome, examined the question of authority to interpret Christian tradition. He discussed the authority of the whole community of the faithful, of the bishops and of theologians, as well as that of councils and of the pope. This discussion, based heavily on the documents of the Second Vatican Council, emphasized the plurality and basis of authoritative voices in church teaching.

What the above-mentioned books demonstrate from positive historical evidence is reinforced by such recent studies of factors limiting hierarchic power — and that of the papacy in particular — as *The Limits of the Papacy* (New York: Crossroad, 1987) by Patrick Granfield, a Benedictine monk and professor at the Catholic University of America. Like most of the books already mentioned, this one appeals very strongly to the logical implications contained in basic statements of Vatican II, primarily those related to the concept of collegiality. This question of collegiality has been the topic of several recent issues of the well-known international journal *Concilium* — *History: Self-Understanding of the Church,* edited by Roger Aubert in 1971, collected essays from many periods of church history and from many local church traditions to show the contrasts in accepted church structures of authority. *The Teaching Authority of the Believers,* edited by J. B. Metz and Edward Schillebeeckx in 1985, makes the point, based on Scripture and tradition, that the laity derive their authority to interpret the faith, not from the hierarchy, but from their baptism into the community of those who live by faith as disciples of Jesus. A third *Concilium* volume dealing with the collegiality issue, *Collegiality Put to the Test,* edited by James Provost and Knut Walf in 1990, is devoted entirely to the collegiality principle among the bishops. Besides these volumes of *Concilium,* a recent collection of essays, *That They*

Might Live, edited by Michael Downey (New York: Crossroad Publishing Co., 1991), develops particularly the aspect of power in the Church and the imperative of structures which not only speak of the authority of the laity, but which effectively empower the laity in a contemporary Church in which they have largely accepted a passive role that is not proper to them.

This matter of collegiality has received so much attention in recent decades because it was proposed in relation to the bishops of the world in the third chapter of *Lumen gentium,* Vatican II's Dogmatic Constitution on the Church, and was then restricted by a note added to that document by request of Pope Paul VI. Both the principle itself and the restrictive interpretation of it stimulated historical, theological and canonical studies. In the case of the bishops, complex organizational questions were involved. But it was soon realized that the principle can be applied at all levels of the institutional Church. If the bishops are expected to reflect, discern and act together, being jointly responsible for evangelization and cooperation in the redemptive transformation of the world, this suggests something about the whole structuring of the life of the Church. It prompts questions about what it means to be the community of the faithful within each diocese, within each parish. It suggests that communal discernment in which all participate actively, looking for the guidance of the Holy Spirit in listening to one another and in sharing their own understanding, is an integral part of being called into the Church and its mission in the world.

When we look at the earliest Church, as portrayed in the Acts of the Apostles, we see a great deal of initiative coming from within the local communities as soon as the good news has been preached and accepted there. Some people have been baptized and have formed a local community around the celebration of the Eucharist. We read of prophetesses and people who speak in tongues, of the local group sending out missionaries to bring the good word to other cities, and of the recently converted Paul discovering a vocation to be an apostle out of his reflection on his own conversion experience. What is very clear in this prototype of Church presented to us in the New Testament as the authoritative norm, is that the whole community and each of its members seeks the guidance of the Spirit which Jesus has bequeathed to his Church. It is understood that in becoming a member of the community one receives the Holy Spirit, which is a spirit of prophecy, of discernment and transformation.

What is equally clear is that for some centuries local Churches not only exercised initiatives in dealing with situations that arose within their own communities, but also intervened in other communities when it was thought, after communal prayer and reflection, that they could be helpful. The *First Letter of Clement* seems to do that, as does the letter of Cyprian of Carthage *On the Unity of the Church,* addressed to the local Church of the city of Rome. The gathering of local synods to decide on difficult issues by praying and trying to come to a general consensus was a similar exercise of leadership within the local communities. It was this kind of movement of initiative from the "grassroots" which led John Henry Newman in his *Rambler* articles (still frequently cited by theologians today) to defend the expression "consulting the faithful in matters of doctrine." There is an important issue here concerning the nature of leadership in the Church. What we see in the early ages demonstrates the pattern of horizontal leadership: leaders of the local Churches are chosen by the members of those local Churches, and their authority is seen primarily as that of expertise — deep knowledge of the life of faith as shown in the whole conduct of one's affairs and relationships.

A rather dramatic change in this pattern can be discerned in the fourth century with the legalization of Christianity and the imperial patronage of the Churches. The fact that bishops began to be called upon for civic functions in the empire, that they were accorded privileges and insignia of imperial authority, and were summoned to ecumenical councils at the behest of the emperors, changed the perception of the role of bishop in the local Church. That authority came to be seen less as one of expertise and more as one of power to command and be obeyed. Within the local Church a hierarchy of command was established and ritual functions came to have a significance that carried differential status. Among the local Churches relationships shifted subtly also. The emperors came to style themselves "bishop of the bishops," "vicar of Christ," and "great bridge-builder" of the tradition (*pontifex maximus*). The patriarchs became leading personages of the empire, and a hierarchy of the universal Church became a significant power structure. The Western, or predominantly Latin, component of the Church had only one patriarchate — Rome; and when the empire fell apart, the West was left with a monarchic, independent church structure. Even so, the history of the Middle Ages is punctuated with further moves to consolidate centralized power. This was often in an effort to correct abuses and to free the Church from domination by secular power.

In spite of the good intentions that often motivated such moves, by the fifteenth century the Church was being described as a complete society (*societas perfecta*) on analogies which equated the institutional structures with secular governments, and which tended to present the institutional structure as the essential being of the Church. The strong protests against this perception of the Church from the fourteenth century onwards, consolidating in some strands of the sixteenth-century reformation movements, only resulted, with the Council of Trent and the Counter-Reformation developments, in an even more centralized and authoritarian mode of church life. This trend received a final boost at the First Vatican Council, so that authoritarian controls and blind obedience came to be seen by both insiders and outsiders as characteristic of Catholicism.

A critical appraisal of this history, and a return to sources in Scripture and in the testimonies of the early Christian centuries, led to a reversal of the trend at the Second Vatican Council. But the implications of the broad lines of collegiality sketched in its documents were by no means foreseen even by those who helped to draft them and by the bishops who voted on them.

Moreover, some Roman officials and some segments of hierarchy, clergy and laity were in profound disagreement with the vision of Church that was projected. The document on the Church passed only after certain compromises were introduced, so that one can quote selectively from *Lumen gentium* to maintain that it simply continues to endorse monarchic, authoritarian structures. It is this component of initial dissent, selective application, and subsequent hesitation about the further implications that emerge, which causes the hidden agenda. There are those who read this whole document except Chapter 3 as poetic and inspirational, but Chapter 3 as strictly theological. Chapter 3 deals with the Church as hierarchic. The other chapters deal with the mystery of the Church, the Church as people of God, the laity as fully the people of God, the call to holiness, the pilgrim state of the Church, and some special topics. Clearly, the reason some well-informed people consider only Chapter 3 as defining the nature of the Church is that they come to the document with the assumption that ecclesiology, the Church's official account of itself, cannot change.

For those who see the document in its entirety as an attempt to describe or define the Church, a changing self-image is both unavoidable and acceptable. It is a question of whether we can allow that the Church is not only *in* history but *of* history. If we accept the latter view, it does not come as an unwelcome shock to find that at various periods in the Church's development it has modeled itself after secular patterns which, at the time, were thought to be the best — or perhaps the only — ones available. The Church of the earliest centuries, suffering sporadic persecution and general contempt, was clearly conscious of its calling to shape a countercultural community, reflecting the freedom in solidarity that belongs to the reign of God. But ever since the Constantinian establishment in the fourth century, the relationship between the worldly structures of power and the Church have been less critical. There has been a tendency to equate humanly constructed patterns of society quite simply with the will of God, and therefore to accept them uncritically.

This tension between a static and a redemptively dynamic view of the nature of the Church runs through the arguments over the basic ecclesial communities of the Third World, over the disagreements in parishes concerning the role of parish councils and lay leadership of all types, over the discernments and decisions that belong to the local Church rather than to the central authority in Rome, over the role of episcopal confer-

ences, and so forth. These are all issues that have to do
with collegiality — that is, with participation in
decision-making and leadership. They are all issues that
involve a reversal of the long, progressive concentration
of power into pyramids of hierarchic authority set
within one another and each having a monarchic peak.
The present preoccupation of theologians with collegiality, reception, episcopal conferences, local theologies and so forth is therefore prerequisite to many
practical issues. For instance, the issue of birth control
or of women priests is seen and argued very differently
by those who assume that the matter is predetermined
and that hierarchic authority has certain access to the
truth about how such an issue is predetermined, and by
those who assume that we must reflect on our cumulative experience as Christians, pray over the issue and
try to come to a consensus — possibly leaving an issue
open to local or personal determination.

One problem with all authoritarian structures is that
they tend to relationships in which all the communication moves down the pyramid and all the attention is
turned upwards. But in the Church this means that the
continuing experience of the community of the faithful
tends to be disregarded, so that the traditions and expectations of the Church become more and more alien and

unintelligible to its members, and these tend either to share the life of the Church passively and marginally, or simply to drift away from membership altogether. It is not possible to have an active and deeply committed church membership based on teachings and a world-view which has little relevance or intelligibility for the world in which the people actually live. For vital and truly redemptive commitment from the faithful, it is necessary that there be room for reflection and initiative at the grass roots, free communication upwards in the organizational structures, and open-minded, respectful attention downwards in the organizational structures.

This issue has also been discussed by some contemporary theologians, such as Patrick Granfield among those mentioned, under the rubric of "subsidiarity." This is the principle, long proclaimed in the social encyclicals of modern popes, that larger and more complex social structures should not take over functions which can be undertaken successfully by smaller, simpler units. The social encyclicals insisted on the principle of subsidiarity chiefly in defense of the rights of the family in the face of increasing interventions by the state. However, these theologians are pointing out that the same principle holds with respect to the functions of the local Church in the face of increasing intervention from Rome, and with respect to the functions of personal conscience in the face of increasingly detailed pronouncements in intimate matters by distant authorities remote from the experiential foundations for the judgment.

While these matters relate to the organizational structures of the Church at every level, they are felt to be more urgent with respect to the Holy See. One reason for this, of course, is the fact that among the functions that have been appropriated to the See of Rome in the course of time is the selection of bishops for the local Churches. This is a function that originally lay with the well-informed discernment of the people of the local community, who either by public acclaim or by more elaborate methods chose their own bishops. When imperial or royal patronage had usurped this right in many places, the papacy intervened aggressively to protect the independence of the Church from destructive secular control. However, the present experience is rather that papal selection of bishops is used as a means to impose Roman views and expectations on local Churches, and to foreclose new insights and adaptations that might arise out of the experience and pastoral needs of particular local communities. To the argument that this transgresses the principle of subsidiarity, those who favor such centralized imposition of bishops on local communities respond that the principle of subsidiarity does not apply to the Church — which brings us full cycle back to the question whether the structures are the divine element in the Church which can neither be changed nor questioned.

It is in the context of this history and these reflections that the issues concerning papal authority and its exercise keep coming up in theological discussion. Oddly enough, the issue is not really papal infallibility but the aura it casts around the ordinary functioning of the Holy See with all its offices and officials. In the constitution *Pastor aeternus* of Vatican I, there were two key points, the first of which concerned the pope's power to command and rule in dioceses other than his own diocese in Rome. Most of the problems and disagreements today concern Chapter 3 of the constitution, which dealt with this matter. In particular, events in recent decades have once again brought to the forefront the question of the pope's intervention in the ordinary authority of a bishop in his diocese. Some very practical pastoral decisions concerning women in non-ordained leadership positions in the local Church, concerning ministry among homosexuals, anti-nuclear protests, lay preaching, participation in church ministry by those who have left the priesthood, and political action by priests and religious, have become occasions for Roman intervention in the way bishops run their own dioceses. These occasions have raised the question whether the bishop in his own diocese is simply a delegate of the pope or whether he has ordinary authority in the strict sense because he is the consecrated leader of the Church. In the earlier centuries, when communities chose their own bishops, this question would not have arisen. It is the historical accumulation of centralized power and the gradual appropriation by Rome of the selection of bishops, made official in the nineteenth century, which gives the impression that the bishops are the delegates of the pope. Such impressions become the background that is eventually taken for granted as beyond question. And it is with assumptions taken from this background that the right and duty of constant detailed supervision and intervention by the Holy See is claimed.

It is rather important to note that most of such interventions are actions of the Holy See — that is, of a large and complex organizational structure — not of the pope in person. The Church of today is so numerous, so widespread geographically, so varied culturally and linguistically, so complex in the various political, economic and social contexts in which local Churches function, that there is no possibility whatever for any one man to be informed and engaged in all the affairs of all local Churches. Hence the congregations and commissions of the Holy See carry on the ordinary business and claim to act with the authority of the pope. The staffs of these bodies tend to form a subculture rather isolated from the experience of Christians and of clergy in the everyday, practical lives and decisions of the local Churches. If it could really be supposed that they have some type of "hot line" to heaven, some special channel of direct revelation about the right answers to pastoral issues arising in all parts of the world, the isolation would not be a problem. But if the nature of the Church's relationship to the Holy Spirit and to the redemptive vision and wisdom of Jesus is (as history suggests) a matter of prayerful communal discernment trying to come to a consensus, then the isolation and one-way communication is really a blocking of the action of the Holy Spirit. It is this realization that has emboldened so many contemporary theologians to raise questions about the intervention of the Roman See in pastoral decisions made by local bishops on the basis of local experience and local discernment.

A similar question has been raised concerning the relationship of the pope and the composite Holy See with a council while in session as well as after a council has dispersed having laid down guiding principles or specific prescriptions. It is no secret that when Pope John XXIII called the Second Vatican Council, there were strenuous efforts made by key figures in the organizational structures of the Holy See at first to prevent the Council from ever taking place and then to preempt what it would decide upon. The prior knowledge of this, combined with good strategy and prompt action on the part of four cardinals, effectively opened real communication and debate so that the Council did not become a rubber stamp for the Vatican officials. It is also a concern, however, that, according to the customary claims and exercise of authority by the Vatican staff, much that was opened up in the Council can be closed up again. One example of this is the regressive rulings in ecumenical matters. Another is the effective restriction of the third rite of reconciliation (the one with general absolution without individual confession) by the Congregation for the Doctrine of the Faith, so that this rite is all but eliminated. A third example is the frequent punitive action against theologians who explore further aspects of the contraception question (which the

Council was stopped from discussing by a peremptory message from Pope Paul VI, and which the post-conciliar commission on the topic left as an open question), or questions about lay initiative and decision-making in the Church. A further concern, similar to the one about the relationship between the Holy See and councils, is that of the now periodic synod of bishops. Should such a body gather in Rome simply to receive the correct answers from the Holy See?

Though the questions just proposed are concerned immediately with the balancing of decision-making power between local bishops and the Holy See, they are of indirect but urgent concern to the laity. If all decisions come from the center of a worldwide Church, they inevitably impose a kind of straightjacket. They cannot respond to the needs and situations of the local Church while maintaining uniformity from a distance. If the local bishop has the discretion and freedom to act in the local Church according to the needs and situations that emerge, there is obviously more opportunity for communal discernment to take place, and for a seriously committed, active local Church to grow. The same may be said for bishops' conferences. Moreover, if the local community can once again regain its voice in the selection of bishops, we may hope for a rebirth of the local

Churches in the spirit of the early centuries. Even without a voice in the selection of their own bishops,
something like this has happened in many Third World
communities among the very poor who have taken the
initiative to build a local Church from the base in the
basic Christian communities. For reasons which will be
clear from the above discussion, these communities
have roused distrust and hostility in spite of their generosity, piety and close resemblance to the communities
of believers in the New Testament.

The second issue dealt with by Vatican I has turned
out to be considerably less consequential, though it
raised more protest and debate. The infallibility of
solemn definitions of church doctrine made by a pope
without assembling a council has not really become a
practical concern because it was explicitly invoked on
only two occasions. Both were vindications of popular
Marian devotions against the impact of secularism and
intellectual scoffers. These definitions may have had a
marginal negative impact on ecumenical efforts, but no
more than that. Vatican I's definition of the popes'
authority to declare and define irreformable teachings is
a source of tension in the contemporary Church, not in
its specific implementation (because the Council itself
hedged that authority about with limits and safeguards),

but in the aura it casts over papal teaching authority, as though it could be equated with divine authority absolutely and beyond question in every detail of every utterance (in a way no longer accorded to the text of Scripture). It is this attitude, founded on assumptions already described in this chapter, which comes into conflict with the Vatican II projection of a vital Christian community engaged in redemptive activity in the world.

Suggestions for Further Reading

The Limits of the Papacy by Patrick Granfield (New York: Crossroad Publishing Co.; London: Darton, Longman & Todd, 1987), though densely packed with fact and argument, is very clear and informative. It is most helpful in the effort to understand why the question of authority of the local Churches has arisen as an urgent one in our times.

Council over Pope? by Francis Oakley (New York: Herder & Herder, 1969) takes a provocative stand in suggesting the logical and historical implications of what happened at the Second Vatican Council. Most readers will especially appreciate the long historical section of this book.

Magisterium: Teaching Authority in the Catholic by Francis A. Sullivan *Church* (New York: Paulist Press; Dublin: Gill & Macmillan, 1983) is more conservative in its approach and suggests a slightly different view of the historical development. Some readers may find it more difficult because of the many allusions and summaries of debate between differing positions.

CHAPTER FOUR

Is the Eucharist Really
Connected with Social Justice?

At the very heart of the Church's self-understanding is the eucharistic gathering of the community. With the implementation of *Sacrosanctum concilium,* the Constitution on the Sacred Liturgy, Catholic piety has made a difficult shift from an individualistic to a communitarian form of eucharistic piety. Moreover, there has been a shift from the cult of unquestioned mystery, reinforced by the use of a sacred language (Latin), an obscure ritual performed on behalf of a passive congregation, and an aura of hushed silence in usually dimly-lit buildings. The shift has been towards a vigorous quest for fuller understanding, through the simplifying of the rites and the introduction of extensive Scripture reading and homiletic commentary, through active involvement of the congregation, different dispositions of the buildings, selection of appropriate hymnody, and so forth.

Many Catholics who have moved through these changes and become accustomed to them, nevertheless find it unreasonable that a link should be proposed between Eucharist and social-justice issues. They have a strong sense that this may be just another fad sweeping the community once it has become used to changes. Yet this connection is as old as the Eucharist itself and goes back to the Hebrew roots of the Eucharist. Of course, Jesus gave us the action at the Last Supper, but little direct theological explanation of the action. If we put the Last Supper discourse in John's Gospel together with the account of the action and words in the three other gospel accounts and that of Paul in I Corinthians, we get some sense that the purpose of what Jesus did and invited them to do was to keep his followers intimately in touch with him and to draw them into a deeper understanding of and sharing in his mission of redeeming the world. His earliest followers seem to have seen some radical consequences as flowing from their participation in his Eucharist. It changed their life-style in quite dramatic ways, as we are told in the Acts of the Apostles, 2:42–47 and 4:32–35. In the course of the next three centuries they achieved some important transformations in society simply by working from the grassroots situation of their own membership. It is the return to the sources of our eucharistic tradition that has shown once again the close connection of Eucharist with social-justice issues in the societies in which we live.

What Jesus did in his farewell meal must have looked very different from our present-day celebration. The context was a family setting in a home among friends. The group was observing a Jewish festival, Passover. His followers were used to Jesus teaching in stories and images, conveying a message by an action and giving new or renewed meaning to traditional symbols, and this he did also at the Last Supper. The Passover liturgy commemorates the liberation of the people of Israel from Egypt, in a reenactment of that unfinished past event which makes it present by the present participation of these people at this time. The great liberation is never complete but is always still going on and still challenging each generation and each person to be part of a transformation in covenant with

God. The transformation is the refocusing of human society to be truly in harmony under the reign of God.

Certainly, Jesus was celebrating the Passover meal in this spirit and investing it with the new meaning of his self-gift for the realization of the reign of God. In the time immediately after the Second Vatican Council there was a great renewal of understanding of what this meant in terms of the formation of a community of believers, going back to the oft-repeated message of Paul that we are called to enter into the death and resurrection of Christ by leaving behind our former way of life and entering into an entirely new kind of life. It has, of course, always been the concern of Christian individuals and Christian communities to try to see more clearly just what kind of new life is meant. The early communities understood that it was to be counter-cultural in its radical sharing both of material goods and of more subtle riches, such as faith and hope and genuine fellowship. With the Constantinian establishment in the fourth and subsequent centuries, there came gradually to be less emphasis on real transformation in the practical patterns of social life and more focus on the individual, on hope after death, and on acceptance of the will of God in a rather static sense which seemed to assume that the existing order in human society could be equated quite simply with his will.

When this more individual and private piety was transferred to the new Christians converted in large masses among the barbarians at the beginning of the Middle Ages, a poorer understanding of the symbolism and narrative foundations of the Christian way of worship led to an almost magical focus on secret words and signs — an understanding that what was important was the doing of exactly the right actions and the saying of exactly the right words by someone endowed with more than ordinary human powers. This drew attention away from the participation of the whole community in the eucharistic assembly, and most of all from concern with the changes that were supposed to follow in the people and in the world in which they were living and acting and relating to one another. That is why we in modern times inherited much discussion over orthodoxy expressed in terms of "transubstantiation" of the gifts on the altar, and considerably less concern with transubstantiation of the world about us to become truly the people of God in the reign of God. Although the shift to this latter concern was already set out in principle in the Constitution on the Liturgy at Vatican II, immediate theological efforts at that time by leading theologians like Karl Rahner and Edward Schillebeeckx were focused on ways of giving contemporary intelligibility to sacramental efficacy. They were concerned to show that the presence of Jesus in the Eucharist and the channeling of grace through the sacraments were not just unintelligible teachings that must be believed, but rather were supposed to make sense and elicit our cooperation in the transformation of human existence that is the redemption.

In more recent writings, such as Schillebeeckx's *Jesus: An Experiment in Christology* (New York: Seabury Press, 1979), the first volume of his trilogy, and even more so in the second volume, *Christ: The Experience of Jesus as Lord* (New York: Crossroad Publishing Co., 1981), there is a further concern which has to do with the nature of the transformation which is the content of our hope and to which the Eucharist is instrumental. In this last, Schillebeeckx writes of the human community in search of a way of life which will overcome suffering, the crucial issues of human solidarity that are raised by Christian faith and discipleship, and the inseparable link between redemption and many kinds of human liberation from oppression, misery and want. In the third volume, *Church: The Human Story of God* (New York: Crossroad Publishing Co., 1991),

Schillebeeckx writes of the universal salvific meaning of the gospel, which is for the whole suffering human race, and not only for the relatively small circles of believers. The eucharistic gathering is the mirror held up to the world, prototype of the solidarity, compassion and common effort that is intended in the divine call to be for others.

The shift in recent sacramental theology towards a more outward-looking expectation and explanation of our worship as Christians and the effect which that worship is supposed to have in our lives and actions, is so pervasive that it is difficult to point to particular authors as primarily responsible. An insightful essay by the Franciscan sacramental theologian Kenan Osborne, professor in the Graduate Theological Union at Berkeley — "Eucharistic Theology Today," in *Alternative Futures for Worship, Vol. 3: The Eucharist,* edited by Bernard Lee (Collegeville, Minn.: The Liturgical Press, 1987) — lists five factors as particularly influential. The first is an increasingly historical understanding of Eucharist; the second, a return to biblical sources for interpretation and understanding of the action; the third, a more existential philosophical foundation; the fourth, the impact of liberation theology; and the fifth, the impact of the ecumenical movement.

How startling the impact of a return to Scripture for
the interpretation of Eucharist can be is well shown in
an essay by the Jesuit theologian John C. Haughey,
"Eucharist at Corinth: You Are the Christ," in *Above
Every Name,* edited by Thomas Clarke. As this essay
shows, Paul's understanding of Eucharist and of the
presence of Christ in the Eucharist focuses sharply on
the social impact which the community's celebration is
intended to have, in the first place on those who are
gathered, and beyond that on the whole of the society
around them. For these Christian communities so near
to the beginning, the hope of salvation was not other-
worldly and remote, to be reached only after death and
outside of history. Their concept of God as creator and
redeemer, ultimately ruler of all, did not allow them to
suppose that economic, political and other public affairs
were quite outside the power, authority and concern of
God.

The ecumenical movement has influenced Catholic
appreciation of the Eucharist not only in encounters and
exchanges with other Christians but, in a special way,
in encounters with Jewish communities and in opportunities to take part in a full Hebrew Passover Seder.
What has become more readily apparent is the direct
connection between the legacy of Jesus to us and the

Exodus as the prototype of all redemption. What Christian use of the Hebrew Scriptures has often obscured is how secular an event the Exodus was. It was a slave revolt by marginalized people who had been driven into servitude by economic factors and were the victims of increasingly oppressive conditions imposed on them by those who were making a profit out of their labor. It began with a consciousness-raising campaign by someone who claimed to have been called by God to oppose the oppressors and demand rights for the victims. It continued with bitter confrontations, robbery of the rich by the destitute, and flight. We have had a tendency so to idealize the story that the raw human experiences and conflicts are carefully distilled into divine vengeance and vindication, and we forget the form in which the divine actions took place — namely, sharp human conflict, and radical social and political revolution.

What Jesus celebrated each Passover throughout his lifetime was the compassion of God for the wretched and the power of God to give life, hope and dignity even to the most oppressed and excluded. It would not be too strong to say that Passover celebrated the realization that God was on the side of the poor, the marginalized and those not enjoying the dignity of full civic standing and participation in their society. God was on

their side, not to compensate them after death, but to
right their wrongs within the socio-political order of this
world. It is today, and was then, the task of the host at
the Passover supper to answer questions about the
meaning of the memorial meal and its various elements.
The purpose was to invite the household and its guests
to enter into the event as a continuing, present transformation, reflecting on their own context and society in
order to ask what yet remained to hope, pray and strive
to change. The ritual makes room for the host to reflect
on this in a kind of homily on the narrative readings and
on the psalms and chants that are part of the evening.
This commentary should ordinarily take in the various
symbolic items on the table.

In commenting on the meaning of the bread which
on this day has not been leavened but is flat and unin-
teresting, the host is given this guideline for improvisa-
tion. There are three things to be said about unleavened
bread in a culture that uses sourdough leavening. Not
only is unleavened bread a sign of haste because the
Hebrews were fleeing in terror of their lives, as so
many refugees are in our own times. Unleavened bread
is also a sign of destitution because it is the homeless —
in those days, the despised desert nomads — who do
not have the facilities for such nice domestic comforts

as kneading the soured old dough into the new, setting it in a well-ventilated, temperature-controlled place to rise slowly, and then baking it in specially constructed ovens. But (and this is the third point) it is precisely because it is the unleavened bread of affliction, the bread of the destitute, homeless and despised, that it is also the bread of a new beginning, a radical break with the past, untrammeled by the established prejudices and injustices. The point of this is that sourdough baking links each batch with all of those before; the leaven becomes a symbol of the way past violent or destructive deeds keep fermenting and creating chains of consequences for the future. There often seems to be a dead-end situation in which there is no hope of escape or breakthrough. Exodus proclaims that with God there is a breakthrough to a new beginning, no matter how desperate the situation, and that it is the destitute, the hopeless, the utterly despised who will be ready to take the risk when God opens the way. God is on the side of the poor, not because they are more virtuous (which they may or may not be in particular cases), but because they are more obviously needy and ready to hear good news and take risks.

All this is contained in the symbolism of the Passover Seder, and into this context Jesus infuses his own meaning, not contradicting but enhancing the message that is already there. He points to his ultimate confrontation leading to his execution by the established powers, and invites his followers to see his death as the breaking and sharing of the unleavened Passover bread. The great breakthrough is going to happen out of the terror, the utter affliction and the ultimate destitution. Similarly, commenting on the wine, which has always carried the symbolism of the shedding of blood, he invites them to see the shedding of his blood in a horrible, quite secular and crude execution, not as an unspeakable event to be forgotten or glossed over and sacralized, but as paradigmatic of the redemption that can spring up out of the most hopeless situations among the most despised.

The early community of the followers of the way of Jesus seems to have grasped the levels of meaning packed into the fact that Jesus extended his presence to them in the context of a shared table fellowship and by an action that linked this immediately to his death. The table fellowship reminds us that we are at all times the guests of God's hospitality in creation and history, and the link with the death of Jesus adds that the hospitality of God as we know it is not only in the order of creation but in an order of redemption, of putting things right that have been distorted and destroyed. When Jesus extends the hospitality of God, what he offers is in the first place himself, and we are invited not only as guests but as fellow hosts. When Jesus extends his presence in the Eucharist, it is not some static, timeless and rather ethereal presence to be contemplated peacefully and gratefully. It is a presence that invites the participants into the decisive moment of his self-gift in death and into all the consequences which that has for the continuing work of the redemption. We are invited to be fully participant in this presence — indeed, in the words of Paul in the New Testament, to become the body (that is, the presence) of Christ redemptively in our world, doing what Jesus does. As one sacramental theologian, Franciscan Regis Duffy, professor in the Washington Theological Union, has pointed out in his book *Real Presence* (New York: Harper & Row, 1982), presence is a reciprocal reality, and it is much more urgent to make sure we are truly present at the Eucharist in its deeper meaning, than to be concerned with just how we are going to explain the presence of Christ.

It is, however, especially in the praxis of basic Christian communities among the poorest of the poor of our contemporary world, that the challenge arises to see the full meaning of Eucharist and its inevitable connection with all issues of unnecessary human suffering, abandonment and oppression. This is not a matter of demands that these groups make on others; much less are they making any accusations against rich classes or rich nations. What they are doing is meditating on the Scriptures in the context of Sunday eucharistic gatherings that look very much like the assemblies of the early Christians on the Lord's Day. Often they include long discussions of what it means in their own context to live by the hope and vision of the gospel, a fellowship meal in which they share their meager resources generously, and a kind of business meeting to help one another in their most urgent needs. Out of this has come, for instance, a remarkable series of books entitled *The Gospel in Solentiname*.

In a more systematic way the connection between the eucharistic gathering and the social issues confronting Christians in the larger society has been formulated by some of the professional theologians whom we know as liberation theologians. Gustavo Gutierrez, for instance, makes the connection in several contexts beginning with his first book, *A Theology of Liberation,* published in English in 1973 (Maryknoll, N.Y.: Orbis Books), two years after its first publication in

Spanish in Peru. His point in the chapter on Eucharist is that this central act of worship is a prophetic gesture, because full communion with God and others (enacted in the Eucharist) is incompatible with any sort of injustice or exploitation. He recalls the gospel saying of Jesus, that anyone bringing a gift to the altar and remembering that a fellow human being has a just grievance, must leave the gift and first go to seek honest reconciliation with that person (Mt. 5:23–24). Even an untutored reflection on the symbolism of the shared table fellowship at Christ's invitation to God's hospitality will bring an awareness of the intrinsic logic of this.

Suggestions for Further Reading

The theme of this chapter has been developed at much greater length in my book *The Eucharist and the Hunger of the World* (recently reissued — Kansas City: Sheed & Ward, 1992). A very bold Asian perspective on the question is presented in *The Eucharist and Human Liberation* by Tissa Balasuriya (Maryknoll, N.Y.: Orbis Books; London: SCM, 1978).

Chapter 12 of *A Theology of Liberation* by Gustavo Gutierrez (Maryknoll, N.Y.: Orbis Books; London: SCM, 1973) is well worth anyone's time to read and reread and meditate upon. Almost any book or essay on the experiences of the basic Christian communities will also illustrate the far-reaching social implications of the celebration of Eucharist. Similarly revealing is *The Gospel in Solentiname,* edited by Ernesto Cardenal (Maryknoll, N.Y.: Orbis Books; London: Darton, Longman & Todd, 1979).

CHAPTER FIVE

Where and How Is the Redemption Happening?

The liberation theologians have focused on the critical question: What do we mean by terms such as *salvation* (the root meaning of which is "healing") and *redemption* (the root meaning of which is "buying back" or "ransoming")? As will be evident from the discussion in the first two chapters, it is a question that tends to uncover the hidden agenda of what we understand as the divine element in the Church, what we see as changeable and entrusted to our communal responsibility, and what we see as the enduring and central reality of the Church. This in turn raises many questions about the sources, nature and exercise of authority in the Church.

It is not surprising therefore that liberation theology has aroused so much opposition, especially from those with a strong stake in the civil or ecclesiastical *status quo*. As with the work of Thomas Aquinas in his own time and of many important and influential scholars in our century who were subsequently vindicated and assimilated into standard church teaching, these authors have raised foundational questions in such a way that more conservative thinkers are afraid the whole structure of the Church's tradition might fall apart. But their warrant for doing this is in the gospel itself applied more logically and less cautiously to the contemporary human situation on a local and worldwide scale.

What the liberation theologians are discussing now really had its beginnings in the work of Henri de Lubac and Karl Rahner on grace. These two authors in their earlier work were also held suspect and treated rather badly when they suggested that grace must make an observable difference in human lives and societies. For Rahner, this was part of the existential movement in theology, trying to see the religious traditions in terms of recognizable human experience, so that our faith would be less alien to our everyday lives and more meaningful in the way we direct them. For de Lubac, a French Jesuit theologian with a strong background in the Church Fathers and the historical development of Christian thought, this conviction about grace was based on Paul's use of the term and notion of grace in the New Testament and on the way that usage was picked up in the Fathers of the Church.

The insight which these two scholars brought forward had some important repercussions on the relationship between what had been called the teaching Church and the learning Church, or the magisterium and the faithful. To put it very crudely, this insight changed the balance of power in the structures of the institutional Church because it implied that holiness and grace were in principle subject to scrutiny by sincere believers, who were therefore less dependent on magisterial direction and sacramental reassurance. For those who saw the core and continuity of the Church in the promise and presence of Jesus and the empowerment of the baptized by the Holy Spirit, drawing them to seek more fully the reign of God in all human affairs, this work on grace was an important step forward in understanding the Christian vocation and responding to it. But for those who identified the divinely guaranteed core and continuity of the Church with the institutional structures, such an understanding of grace threatened the hold that the structures had on the conduct of the members in all aspects of their lives, and as such it threatened the Church itself.

Fortunately, the Second Vatican Council endorsed this understanding of grace in several of its documents by the way it addressed the tasks of the Church in the world, the basis of ecumenism, and the vocation of the laity, among other issues. But the further implications drawn out, for instance, in the work of J. B. Metz on political theology, were again resisted point by point, because they seemed to secularize the Christian vocation in ways that made the whole project of the Church less tidy and less easily controlled from the center. It must be emphasized that it is not necessary to presume self-interest on either side. The progressive theologians were writing out of a very different experience of Church and world than the experience of the more conservative forces that opposed them. Nor is it necessary to presume intellectual superiority on one side or the other. It seems less a matter of consistent argument and clear thinking than of the presence or absence of certain radicalizing experiences in one's life. There is a very coherent logic on both sides, but it is based on differently contextualized experience of human existence.

It is onto this battlefield of lines already drawn that the liberation theologians arrived as the latest contingent on the progressive side, meeting a conservative force already on the alert for anything that might threaten the integrity and security of its position. These liberation theologians came with the simplicity and humility of spokespersons like Gustavo Gutierrez but also with the feisty impact of others like the martyr Ignacio Ellacuria. And their message was that we all need to be far more honest in recognizing that liberation from sin is not a matter of celestial accounting but very much a matter of terrestrial transformations in the way we treat one another, not only on a face-to-face, one-to-one basis, but also in the way we structure our economies and our societies to give some segments of the human community privileged participation and consumption while others are marginalized and deprived. One would not expect this to be a welcome message to the powerful, privileged and wealthy, and indeed it was not well received by any of these groups.

As explained in a recent book by Philip Berryman, *Liberation Theology* (New York: Pantheon Books, 1987), liberation theology is an interpretation of Christian faith out of the experience of the poor. Of course, the poor do not write the books or work out the systematic explanations. That is done by trained theologians who have spent much of their working lives in dialogue with the poor, living among them and in solidarity with them. This puts these theologians into a position very much like that of Jesus himself, who spent his public life bringing the good news to the poor peasantry in a conquered and oppressed nation whose whole economy and politico-religious life suffered from its subordination to the imperial interests of Rome. When theology is done from the experience of the poor, one of the significant aspects that emerges is the realization that it is not enough to speak of the redemptive death of Jesus as the center of our faith and the model for Christian piety, without locating that death in relation to his life and ministry, to the content of his preaching, the focus of his miracles, and the values and hopes for which he was willing to sacrifice himself. What emerges clearly is that Jesus was not crucified by divine edict unrelated to the concrete circumstances of his ministry and of the social and political context in which it was carried out.

Liberation theology is based on the understanding that poverty is not accidental, but is the outcome of the way the human community organizes itself. That organization, and all the human decisions which go to make it up, come under moral and spiritual scrutiny. They are not outside the responsibility that we have to God our creator and to Jesus our Savior. They come within the scope of the redemption because, no matter how complex the structures of society, in the last analysis they are a matter of how we treat one another, whether we really love our neighbor as ourselves, and whether we are committed to the common good and the realization of God's reign among us.

Because action on behalf of the suffering, the poor and the oppressed or marginalized must be effective to be genuinely redemptive, it moves the sense of discipleship into the public arena as well as into our immediate relationships. Hence, interpretation of the faith from the experience of the poor means a critique of society with its structures and its ideologies, and a self-critique of the Church's ministry with the question whether the official activity of the Church springs entirely from the same concerns which Jesus manifested in his lifetime. It should be stressed, because objections along these lines are so frequently voiced, that no liberation theologians suggest it is possible or even desirable for society to assure that everyone has exactly the same. They do not expect equality; but, according to a teaching that was very strong in the Church until the twelfth century, they insist that we all hold our wealth in trust, so to speak, from God, for the benefit of those who need it. This

refers especially to wealth that can be invested to
become productive, and in modern times it has very
significant implications for investment, taxation, tariff,
subsidy and other economic policies. There are ways of
organizing society and its economy that favor technical
progress, national prestige and power, and the gross
national product, but at the cost of leaving sections of
the population behind in ever-increasing deprivation,
misery and humiliation, or at the cost of driving less
competitive nations into dire want and mass starvation.
Modern technology, communications, and socio-
economic analysis have lifted these trends and forces
out of the realm in which patterns of causality were not
understood into the clear light. With this, we as a
people have emerged from a cocoon of relative
innocence with respect to these larger issues into an
inescapable condition of responsibility for decisions
made in our behalf in democratic societies. What this
means, then, is not that everyone should be equal but
that none should be left out, that no classes or populations should be held in contempt or disregard, and that
no groups should be forced into conditions of brutaliz-
ing want or mass death by starvation and disease when
ample resources and possibilities exist in the world to
resolve such conditions. A Church concerned with the

concerns of Jesus should remember that he said that those with two coats should give one to the person who is without.

Many of those who have raised objections to the liberation theologians' analysis of the redemption in our world today and of the role that the Church should be playing, have written that the matter is not as simple as set forth above. The Church, they say, has always recognized that coaxing people out of their selfishness and lack of compassion is part of its work, and that this certainly relates directly to the redemption. But, they maintain, this should be done by appeal to the conscience and compassion of those with power and wealth; it should never arouse conflict, resentment or envy, much less involve any violence. Here again, it must be made clear that there is not one liberation theologian who advocates violence, envy or resentment. They do, however, suggest — as in *Jesus Christ, Liberator* by Leonardo Boff (Maryknoll, N.Y.: Orbis Books, 1978) and *Christology at the Crossroad* by Jon Sobrino (Maryknoll, N.Y.: Orbis Books, 1976) — that the model proposed to us in the gospel accounts of the ministry and preaching of Jesus is not a nonconflictual model. Jesus confronts bullying power and oppression by asserting the dignity and human freedom of the oppressed peasant classes, and from time to time he accuses those who exercise power oppressively in blunt terms within the hearing of the poor, modeling for them a fearless assertion of their human rights and dignity as God's people in face of any threat of reprisal and repression.

The common claim of the liberation theologians in their understanding of the redemption and of the appropriate action of the Church and of individual Christians is that it is integral to the task not to promote violence, but to unmask the violence that is already there because it is counter to the reign of God in human society. We have become so used to the progressive impoverishment and periodic mass starvation of the human race, that even when Pope Paul VI issued the encyclical *Populorum progressio* (On the Development of Peoples) in 1967, many Catholics deemed it irrelevant to his role as pope and considered themselves entitled to ignore it, while the *Wall Street Journal* (ordinarily careful of offending religious sensibilities) had no hesitation in ridiculing and denouncing it as "warmed-over Marxism." Pope Paul VI's proposals concerning Third World mass suffering received this response even though the document simply appealed for voluntary common action and avoided any discussion of conflict.

The business world, however, understands very clearly that human economies are not nonconflictual, but a struggle for markets, wealth and bargaining power. Any empowerment of those hitherto excluded changes the balance of power so that those formerly privileged have to yield some privilege. It is the uses of existing economic and political power to prevent any such change in the balance of power, by which the marginalized and excluded would gain a foothold and be able to participate, which constitutes the hidden violence that is already there. The liberation theologians do not advocate that the poor should take up guns but that they should learn to organize themselves cooperatively and gain bargaining power, and that the Church should be on their side, helping them to do so. Where the clergy and religious have been doing this, chiefly in Latin America, we regularly hear of their being murdered by those defending existing privilege; we do not hear of this happening in reverse.

There has been considerable misunderstanding of the liberation theologians' use of the term *revolution*. In the English-speaking world, we tend to associate the word with killing and a take-over of political power by physical violence. However, what the theologians have in mind would be closer to the industrial revolution — a turning around of the economic and social relationships and structures by which society enables people to make a living, support their families, settle in a home and build a way of life for themselves and their neighbors. The theologians are looking for another revolution of that kind with the objectives of including those now excluded in such a way that they can fulfill all those human and social functions with true human dignity, and contribute to, as well as enjoy, the common good. In this sense, they point out, the preaching and impact of Jesus was revolutionary, as documented in the early chapters of the Acts of the Apostles. The revolution that Jesus preached and envisaged was already adumbrated in much of the Hebrew Scriptures, in the laws concerning land ownership, forgiveness of debtors after a certain time, access to the gleaning of fields, the treatment of day laborers and those in servitude, and much else. The revolution that is envisaged is one that radically transforms, or turns around, human patterns of relationship towards that harmony which is the result of God's reigning in human affairs. And this is the concern of the redemption.

Suggestions for Further Reading

With the liberation theologians one can begin almost anywhere because they are all at pains to lay out the historical and biblical foundations for their position. Certainly the most influential book and the first one to be available in English was *A Theology of Liberation* by Gustavo Gutierrez (Maryknoll, N.Y.: Orbis Books; London: SCM, 1973).

A very helpful secondary source is *Theology for a Liberating Church* by Alfred Hennelly (Washington: Georgetown University Press, 1989). It is relatively short, very clear, and gives the text of the Vatican Instruction *On Christian Freedom and Liberation* as well as an excellent and balanced chapter commenting on the Instruction and helping the reader to see it in its context.

Extensive historical background on the structure and spirituality of the Latin-American Churches and their "colonial Christianity" as shaping the need and the actual occurrence of liberation theology and its searching questions is offered in *History and the Theology of Liberation* by Enrique Düssel (Maryknoll, N.Y.: Orbis Books, 1976).

CHAPTER SIX

What Is Sin?

Some have objected that the reflections on the redemption as summarized in the previous chapter seem to do away with sin, or at least secularize the concept and distance it from the responsibility of the individual person. The concept of sin is as much as ever an integral part of the Christian understanding of the human situation. The Christian gospel is the good news that the world as we know it — with all its sufferings and injustices and deprivations for so many people — is not the world as God intends and promises it to us. It is the more complex reality of God's good world, in part cultivated in response to God's call and in part distorted by human selfishness and greed. The distortion that is there is the sin and sinfulness from which we need to be redeemed, and from which we are being redeemed, by Jesus and by all the good impulses he has set in motion in history. The message of redemption does not have any meaning except in the context of a view of the human situation as distorted by initiatives and values that are counter to God's intent for the world.

It is, however, this concept of social sin, appearing in recent church documents as well as in writings of theologians, which is a problem to many believers. Because they connect the concept of sin inseparably with the idea of personal guilt for something freely chosen, they see the notion of social sin and the idea of sinful structures as quite simply absurd. No individual can be assigned the blame for larger injustices and distortions in society. "People sin, not society or structures" has been the slogan of those who have protested against the very idea. At the same time, the objectors usually accept the idea of original sin as an important doctrine of the Church, connect it with the Genesis story and do not think further about it.

The groundwork for the contemporary understanding of social sin and the challenge of sinful structures was really laid by a number of biblical scholars, such as

André-Marie Dubarle in *The Biblical Doctrine of Original Sin* (reissued in English, New York: Herder & Herder, 1964) and one very important systematic theologian, the Dutch Jesuit Piet Schoonenberg, in his four-volume work later condensed into the single volume translated under the title *Man and Sin* (Notre Dame: University of Notre Dame Press, 1965). In that book, Schoonenberg looked at the development of the concept of original sin in Christian writings from the time of Paul in the New Testament, and ended with the question: Does the term really refer to the cumulative sin, sinfulness and distortion of the human situation in history?

Today believers are not as shocked at this idea as they were when these authors first raised it. It has become more generally acknowledged that the original storytellers, scribes and compilers of the book of Genesis were not relating the story of two people in the dim distance of prehistory, but were interpreting the human situation in which each of us is placed. In particular, each of us comes into the progressively more independent use of a free will in the context of what we learn from others in an already rather confused world. We learn the difference between right and wrong in a society that has blurred this difference in many cases by prejudices, by long-term injustices in society which are taken for granted, by forms of violence which have been institutionalized so that we do not see them, and by much more of the same type. Because we acquire our standards of right and wrong within a society that holds these distortions, we are drawn into false relationships and values through no fault of our own. It takes a very highly developed critical consciousness to evaluate the things that one's own society holds to be true or takes as the inevitable order of human relationships. Living by these accepted standards is something that is not the fault of the individual, yet the individual needs to be redeemed from such a life. Where there is no fault there may nevertheless be responsibility to do something about it, to bring about a change.

Some have objected that this does not seem to correspond closely enough with the traditional definition of original sin, because the authoritative church teaching has insisted that sin is not only in the world about us but in every person from the first moment of that person's existence, even before birth. To equate original sin with historical distortion of values and judgments about human situations, seems at first sight to contradict the traditional insistence on the involvement of every human being from the first moment of existence. However, it may be helpful to reflect on what we are at the first moment of existence, and indeed long after that. We are basically living organisms with immense potential to develop language and thought, individual initiative, judgment and action. But the only way any of the potential can be developed is by what others do for us and to us, directing, welcoming and guiding our interaction with the world. Because each of us is dependent in that way, the individual's potentiality is crippled or marred by whatever distortions exist in society. It seems likely that the emphasis on the involvement of each and all in original sin was sustained throughout Christian history so that believers would learn to be self-critical of the values and expectations they take for granted — the values that the prevailing ethos of the society endorses.

What is perhaps a new insight in the recent literature referring to "social sin" is the understanding that many of these distortions are quite beyond the power of the individual to challenge, no matter how clearly that individual may be involved in a radical Christian conversion. What have been called "sinful structures" really need to be unmasked and shown for what they are in a way that the whole society can recognize. Such structures and accepted values change slowly, but they are not unchangeable. They begin to change out of a process of consciousness-raising among all those involved. That raising of critical consciousness has to come from somewhere, from some insight and initiative that transcends the ordinary life and thought of the society. In other words, sin has to be revealed; it is not spontaneously recognized.

Earlier works of J. B. Metz, especially his essay "The Future in the Memory of Suffering," reprinted in a number of collections, pointed out that the crucifixion of Jesus is redemptive in history in the first place because it unmasks the hidden sinfulness in structures, laws, values and expectations of society generally taken for granted and seen uncritically. This theme reemerges in the liberation theologians — for instance, in Jon Sobrino's *Jesus in Latin America* (Maryknoll, N.Y.: Orbis Books, 1982), and again in his essay "The Crucified Peoples: Yahweh's Suffering Servant Today" in the *Concilium* volume *1492–1992: The Voice of the Victims,* edited by Leonardo Boff and Virgil Elizondo (Philadelphia, Pa.: Trinity Press International, 1990). The contention in these writings is that the Church's meditation on the crucified Christ should lead to an awareness that social behavior and apparently sound and acceptable ways in which human society regulates relations among people can never be beyond scrutiny and suspicion. From there, this meditation should lead further to the recognition of many other sufferers for whom Jesus has become a revelatory prototype, and with whom he has irrevocably identified himself in order to show the sinful distortion of the social order which causes their suffering.

This distortion of the social order is what has been named social sin, because the distortion arises out of human actions and decisions of the past and can be changed, with the help of grace, by human action in the present and in the future. How deeply this understanding is rooted in our tradition is clearly demonstrated by William J. Walsh and John P. Langan in the essay "Patristic Social Consciousness — the Church and the Poor," and by David Hollenbach in the essay "Modern Catholic Teachings Concerning Justice." Both these essays appear in the volume *The Faith That Does Justice,* edited by John C. Haughey (New York: Paulist Press, 1977). The extent to which the concept of social sin is biblically rooted is illustrated, for instance, in the essay "Sin and the Powers of Chaos" by Bernard Anderson in the volume *Sin, Salvation and the Spirit,* edited by Daniel Durken (Collegeville, Minn.: The Liturgical Press, 1979).

Perhaps the most interesting development of all, however, is the extent to which the concepts of social sin and sinful structures have become explicit in the writings of Pope John Paul II. He used the terms specifically in the encyclical letter *Sollicitudo rei socialis* (On Social Concerns, no. 36) issued in 1988, and in *Reconciliatio et paenitentia* issued in 1984. This explicit usage of the vocabulary emerging from contemporary socio-critical theologies also represents a logical development of issues and analyses appearing in Pope John Paul II's own earlier encyclical *Laborem exercens* (On Human Work) issued in 1981, and in the encyclical letters of several of his predecessors.

A number of recent writers have also pointed specifically to the Eucharist as a critique of structures — a realization that has arisen out of the renewal of the rites and out of greater interest in the historical development of the Eucharist. Some of these were discussed in Chapter 4. More directly connected with the line of development discussed here is the reflection by Dermot A. Lane in the chapter entitled "The Eucharist and the Praxis of Social Justice" in his book *Foundations for a Social Theology* (New York: Paulist Press, 1984).

Not only in the development of eucharistic theology, but also in the theology and practice of the sacrament of reconciliation has the notion of social sin come to the fore. The very existence of the communal rites of reconciliation points to a need for communal repentance based on communal discernment of sin. The rite of individual confession has traditionally been based on an examination of conscience which recalled specific actions and tried to determine the degree of culpability. This in turn was understood to depend on the clarity of knowledge about the nature and sinfulness of the acts, their actual destructive character, and the extent to which the acts were freely chosen. The modern Catholic sense of sin was closely linked to the experience of preparing to confess sins in the sacrament of penance. But this focus on degrees of personal culpability for specific actions could be pursued to the point of neurotic scrupulosity, while motives and intentions still eluded the penitent in any case. More seriously, this process could be continued on a life-long basis simultaneously with sheer blindness to one's own participation in the prejudices, injustices, oppressions and violence of one's society.

In sharp contrast to this stands the consciousness of sin expressed in documents of the early Christian communities. Their awareness of sin was shaped by the sacramental practice of baptism of adults, and by the experience of the evident contrast between the life of pagan society and life in the Christian community. They wrote of it as a crossing over from death to life, from darkness to light, and from chaos to meaning and purpose, as well as the crossing from a realm of sin to that of the saving grace of Christ. They were speaking of an observable contrast in the structuring not only of individual lives but of relationships and societies of people. Hence for them, sin was not in the first place a matter of specific actions, but a matter of a state of disorientation, a social and personal pattern of distortion.

It is this sense of sin which contemporary theology is at pains to recover. The communal celebration of the sacrament of reconciliation gives scope for this. It allows not only for an examination of conscience to identify specific destructive actions, but also for readings and homilies which propose critical evaluation of harmful aspects of contemporary life and society. The communal celebration not only asks whether we are living according to our understanding of the demands of the Christian life, but also challenges us as to whether that understanding is adequate. The question is not only whether we are keeping the commandments but whether we are living redemptively, which involves discernment and creativity, and certainly demands continuing growth in understanding. What is required is a constant broadening of the horizons and constant attention to new situations and changing conditions.

What this means is that the critical distinguishing factor of the sin from which we need to be redeemed is, not personal culpability, but disorientation from God's reign in our lives and our society. Although we are not personally guilty of many things that are unjust, destructive, or dehumanizing in our society, it is clear that we need to be redeemed, or converted, from involvement in those things. We may have no culpability and yet have responsibility to do something about them. Culpability looks back and tends to be inhibiting and discouraging; responsibility looks forward and is energizing and empowering. In the public life of Jesus as told in the Gospels, there are many incidents in which Jesus tries to redirect the attention of his disciples or of individuals whom he heals away from blame for the past and towards a new direction for the future. It is this spirit that the new communal celebration of reconciliation captures, moving beyond a sense of hopeless repetition into a recognition that we have a place in the history of redemption, and that evil situations can really change. In this sense, the revelation of sin is good news, because it means that those things which are

wrong with our world are not inevitable and unchangeable but can be overcome in the process of redemption.

This kind of scrutiny and the consequent action
depend basically on a vision of the reign of God as the
intended condition of the world, and the promise of its
attainability in God's time and in God's way, but with
our intelligent and freely given cooperation. This concept of the reign (or kingdom) of God in Scripture and
tradition has continued to be a topic for theological
reflection. Benedict T. Viviano, a Dominican professor
at the Ecole Biblique in Jerusalem, has traced the history of this concept through the Christian centuries in
his book *The Kingdom of God in History* (Wilmington,
Del.: Michael Glazier, Inc., 1988), in which he also
provides a bibliography showing the remarkable continuing interest in the idea. The notion that a progressive
vision of God's reign as the projected endtime is being
revealed to us in history has been a powerful focus for
all the socio-critical theologies — the theology of hope,
political theology, various liberation theologies, and so
forth. And this leads to an understanding of sin that is
not so much based on the past and on the keeping of
explicit commandments, but rather is based on the
future and on the contrast between our present and the

future which Jesus has initiated for us but which is yet to be realized in its fulness and all its implications.

In the light of that, a pervasive conviction can be seen in much contemporary theology that suffering — and more particularly avoidable mass suffering — is the key that leads to the recognition of sinful structures, values, expectations and relationships. The vision of the reign of God suggests that the goods of the earth are intended to serve the needs of all, and that God does not create surplus people to be cast off as wastage, nor create some people simply as instruments for the service and enrichment of others. Where people are marginalized, impoverished, humiliated or oppressed by the social system, there is social sin.

Suggestions for Further Reading

The best approach to the notion of "social sin" may be through the *Concilium* volume *1492–1992: The Voice of the Victims* (Philadelphia: Trinity Press International, 1990).

Contemporary perspectives on sin in general are well summarized in *An American Catholic Catechism,* edited by George J. Dyer (New York: Seabury Press, 1975), Part IV: Living the Christian Life. The biblical foundation for a fuller sense of sin is given in *Sin: Biblical Perspectives* by Eugene Maly (Dayton, Ohio: Pflaum Press, 1973). The contemporary reasoning behind the shift in the sense and the definition of sin is set out by David Hollenbach in "Fundamental Theology and the Christian Moral Life," in *Faithful Witness,* edited by Leo O'Donovan and T. Howland Sanks (New York: Crossroad Publishing Co.; London, Geoffrey Chapman, 1989). However, this chapter can be difficult reading. Many of the same ideas emerge in a simpler way in several of the essays in *Concilium* 190: *The Fate of Confession,* edited by Mary Collins and David Power (Edinburgh: T. & T. Clark, Ltd., 1987).

CHAPTER SEVEN

How Does Jesus Save?

An important part of the contemporary agenda in theology has to do with the nature of salvation and the role of Jesus in salvation. This is, of course, the logical counterpart of the discussion on the true understanding of the concept of sin. Salvation, or redemption, is the rescue from sin; therefore the characteristic contexts and categories in which we think about sin will correspond to the characteristic contexts and categories in which we think about salvation. The question about the nature of salvation and the role of Jesus in it is not new, and it is being asked in ways that return to the sources in

Scripture and tradition at the same time that the starting point is in contemporary experience.

During much of Christian history, the emphasis in theological reflection on the role which Jesus plays in our history has been on the claim that he is divine while being fully human. Beginning with that assertion, and going through much argumentation as to the way this could be true, it seemed to require little further explanation that Jesus was therefore the point of reconciliation between the human community and God, bringing the straying creation back to its creator. So the great patristic writers argued for the exchange, and the Council of Ephesus in 431 ruled that one could ascribe divine attributes to Jesus and human attributes to the divine Word. But less attention was paid to any concrete examples of the difference this might make to the human community in history.

There may have been two reasons for this. One was certainly that, from the fourth century onwards, there was less concern with the redemption going on in the world and a great deal more concern with salvation of the individual beyond death. Even the expectation of the Second Coming, which was such a focus of Christian hope and striving in the earliest centuries, had become by the Middle Ages a matter of great dread. But perhaps a more important reason for not paying much attention to any specific expectations of change in history was the tendency to focus on the reasons for the death of Jesus as redemptive. That Jesus saved us by his death is a conviction found as early as the letters of Paul in the New Testament. It was being said by people who were well aware of the entire context, and were making the point that the execution of Jesus was not the defeat of everything he stood for, but something he voluntarily underwent in pursuit of his goals. But subsequent history tended to lose sight of the context.

The development of this focus on the death of Jesus as redemptive has an interesting history which has affected the way the discussion is taking place in our time. Irenaeus, towards the end of the second century, developed the imagery of Jesus in his death paying the ransom to the devil. It was a good image. Putting right what has been distorted always carries a price; it is not literally a matter of paying someone, but it costs some sacrifices and we speak metaphorically of paying the price. Much later, however, Anselm of Canterbury at the end of the eleventh century returned to the traditional expression and declared that the death of Jesus could not be ransom paid to the devil, because the devil could not acquire rights against God by his own wrongdoing.

That led Anselm to speak of the suffering and death of Jesus as compensation paid to the infinite majesty of God for the insult represented by human sin. Anselm did insist that this was not simply imposed on Jesus by the Father, but that Jesus fully agreed to pay this compensation. However, this way of explaining the matter, which became popular in theology, catechesis and piety, had several unfortunate consequences which still haunt us today. Not the least of these is an image of God as vengeful rather than compassionate. Another disadvantage is that all the particular circumstances of the life of Jesus which precipitated his death become irrelevant to discipleship. The believer is not encouraged to understand the confrontations that took place in the public ministry, nor to ask what they mean for the mission of Christians in the world. A third consequence is that Jesus is seen as effectively redemptive in his passivity; independently of circumstances, he had to suffer this terrible death in order to pay the appropriate compensation. It is true that Anselm and subsequent writers admitted that, because of who Jesus was, even some small action on his part would have sufficed to pay the compensation, but they stated further that God preferred it this way because it emphasized the heinousness of all sin. This still left Jesus the model of passivity as the properly devout and obedient posture in the world when confronted with the ambiguities of human society.

It is at this point that many of the contemporary Christologies take issue with the established assumptions. Not only do they deny that the transcendent God revealed by Jesus is appropriately presented in this way of thought, but they also maintain that the self-revelation of Jesus as the realization of the truly human is badly distorted in such a picture. It suggests that we can live a fully human life, fulfilling our responsibility to God, following our vocation, without having to discern what is right or redemptive in the particular situation in which we are placed. There is a kind of disregard for reality and its demands in the presentation. Moreover, the image derived from that argument of Anselm suggests that we are better disciples of Jesus, acting in a more Christian way, if we accept passively, unquestioningly, whatever is going on in our society.

What is common to most contemporary writers on Christology is the conviction that the death must be understood in relation to the life and to the preaching which indicated what Jesus stood for in his own time. Thus Edward Schillebeeckx in his great three-volume masterpiece, *Jesus* (1979), *Christ* (1981), and *Church* (1991), maintains: first, that the concrete historical

circumstances and actions of the life of Jesus are critical
to our entire understanding of our faith; secondly, that
we can reconstruct far more of the historical Jesus and
his impact than has generally been acknowledged since
the nineteenth century; and thirdly, that the political
structures and maneuverings of the Roman occupying
power, the internal Jewish regime, and the relations
between the two, are all immediately germane to an understanding of the decisions that Jesus took and the
stance he maintained.

In following through this line of inquiry, Schillebeeckx comes to a far more critical and active image of
the role Jesus played in the particular context of con-
quest, oppression and impoverishment of his people.
From this, Schillebeeckx also draws important conclusions about the meaning and demands of discipleship in
our time, and about the role of the Church in contemporary society both in its structuring of itself and its internal activities and in its action for the entire world.

What this shift in emphasis has meant in the first
place is a much greater interest in all that can be
retrieved or reconstructed about the historical Jesus and
his context. For many decades there has been research
into the Jewish customs, laws, schools of piety,
legends, rabbinic teachings and so forth which con-

tributed to the cultural context in which Jesus lived and taught. His own characteristic approaches and positions have been more narrowly defined by looking at comparisons and contrasts with what others were doing and saying. But in more recent decades attention has focused on the political aspects with which he dealt, on a more contextualized and nuanced understanding of his relationships with various persons in positions of authority, on the laws, Roman and Jewish, as well as on his attitudes to the economic structures and problems of his time.

Most concretely, this theme has emerged in the writings of socio-critical theologians. Among Catholic theologians it was particularly J. B. Metz in his various essays on "political theology" who led the way in pointing to the identification of the crucified Jesus with all the oppressed, but particularly with the voice of protest against oppression. In his early work *A Theology of Liberation,* Gustavo Gutierrez, Peruvian theologian and practical protagonist for the poor and oppressed, showed how much this more historically concrete understanding of the redemption initiated by Christ had already influenced the Second Vatican Council, especially in its document *Gaudium et spes* (On the Church in the Modern World), and how the

Medellin Conference of the Latin-American bishops in
1968 had effectively accepted the designation of Christ
as liberator in the many dimensions that go to make up
human life. The Brazilian theologian Leonardo Boff, in
his book *Jesus Christ the Liberator* (Maryknoll, N.Y.:
Orbis Books, 1978), devotes a good deal of space to
the issue of what the historical Jesus really wanted to
bring about, noting in passing how much the answers
depend on how we ask the questions. What is inescapable, however, is that Jesus was preoccupied with
the realization of the reign (or kingdom) of God, and
that this is not a "territory" but a new order in society.
This reign of God is to be expected not only in people's
minds but in all aspects of their lives, relationships and
social structures and values. It is the projection of a
revolution in the sense of a radical and pervasive change
in the way we order things among ourselves in every
aspect of our existence together on earth. Most particularly, after presenting Jesus as the champion of the poor
and oppressed, calling for a new order, Boff shows the
death of Jesus as the direct outcome of the message he
preached and the stance he took, pointing out that Jesus
was accused (unjustly, but because of his championing
of the poor) of being what we should call a guerilla
leader and organizer.

Along similar lines, Juan Luis Segundo, in a five-volume Christology, systematically criticizes classic and standard Christologies for their failure to ask questions about the meaning of Jesus and the goals and purpose of his mission in the concrete historical context of his actions, with the realization that in his own context he stood with the poor among a conquered and marginalized people. Jon Sobrino, Jesuit theologian and sole survivor (because he happened to be absent then) of the martyred community at the University of San Salvador, in his book *Christology at the Crossroads* (Maryknoll, N.Y.: Orbis Books, 1978), also focuses on the concept of the kingdom of God as preached by Jesus, its relationship to sin, and the concern with liberation in history. In a later book, *Jesus in Latin America* (Maryknoll, N.Y.: Orbis Books, 1987), he develops these connections further, most especially in terms of what we know of the attitudes of Jesus to the poor, and in terms of the kind of piety and discipleship that should be encouraged among the poor if the preaching and actions of the historical Jesus are taken seriously.

The impact of these writings by the liberation theologians has been extensive and intensive in spite of earlier ridiculing of their positions and their work. The cumulative effect of biblical, historical and systematic reviews of our traditional Christology, and particularly of our traditional ways of explaining how Jesus redeems or saves, has been to raise serious questions that were simply overlooked for many centuries. These questions cannot easily be pushed aside. If the historical Jesus had a different understanding of the reign of God from that which we have attributed to him, we are bound to take notice and adjust our views — no matter how well established — to his. If Jesus was not in fact moving steadily through a preordained pattern of life towards the crucifixion in which he would lavishly pay the penalty of sin to appease the slighted majesty and justice of God, but rather was attempting a peaceful revolution in human society to bring it back under the harmonizing and welcoming reign of God, then our most important concern as Christians is to understand the nature and demands of that peaceful revolution and to continue to play our own part in striving to bring it about. This suggests that concern with matters of social justice, peace, overcoming of cycles of drought and famine, provision of health and livelihood for all, and the drawing of the marginalized into full participation in society and its benefits, are all matters which form the central substance of Christian discipleship, rather than being good works of a marginal and optional kind.

In answer, then, to the question of how Jesus saves, contemporary Christologies shy away from explanations that are detached from real change in human society. They also want to avoid explanations that would have Jesus doing something for everyone else which his followers passively receive. Nor do they want to present the relationship between the humanity and the divinity of Jesus as one in which the role of his humanity is simply to accept unquestioningly and to suffer. They do not want to present the suffering of Jesus or of anyone else as something good and valuable in itself, but rather as something to be overcome if possible or to undergo as the price of some positive move towards the reign of God. They do not deny the nobility of people who are patient in sufferings that cannot be avoided, and they extol the heroism of those who are martyred for their championing of the poor and the oppressed; but they contend that no one has the right to preach in the name of Christ, telling the oppressed that their oppression is the will of God. What has to be spoken in the name of Christ is the message of Christ himself — namely, that oppression is sin and that the will of God is redemption from sin, and therefore liberation from oppression.

Jesus saves, then, not by substituting for the responsibility and activity of other human beings, nor by directing our attention away from what is going on in the world around us, but by instilling the vision and hope of the reign of God which is coming and is always at hand, and by initiating in his own life and ministry a movement that must gain impetus through the ages and the generations. This is a movement of reconciliation in the more profound sense, not of covering up problems and tensions, but of confronting and resolving the injustices and deprivations that are at the heart of all hostilities. It is, moreover, a movement that requires not only unselfishness, dedication and goodwill, but also intelligent analysis of the factors and chains of causality that bring about want and marginalization and every kind of suffering in our world in each age and society. This is always a continuing task, and it has new dimensions in new situations.

It will be said, and it has been said, that this seems to be a very reductionist understanding of the redemption. Two points should be made in answer to this accusation. First, this contemporary emphasis is an attempt to redress the balance against tendencies which etherealized the redemption to the point that practical compassion and responsibility scarcely featured in it.

Secondly, neither Schillebeeckx, nor the liberation theologians, nor any of the principal scholars involved in biblical and systematic refocusing on the reign of God in the preaching of Jesus, deny the transcendent element of the promises — the understanding that the promises of God stretch beyond our scrutiny and in some way transcend death. But the concern of these authors is to redirect our attention from speculation about the beyond to a response to the gospel in the present, in the world, and in the concrete.

Suggestions for Further Reading

A seminal essay of Karl Rahner on the process of redemption is "The Order of Redemption with the Order of Grace," in *The Christian Commitment* (London and New York: Sheed & Ward, 1963). It is an essay which the non-specialist reader will not find too difficult to follow. Another very influential essay is "The Future in the Memory of Suffering" by J. B. Metz, in *Concilium* 76: *New Questions on God* (New York: Herder & Herder, 1972), a volume which Metz also edited. The essay is difficult but rewarding of the effort to understand it.

More easily readable than either of the above are the Christologies of several of the liberation theologians, especially *Jesus in Latin America* by Jon Sobrino (Maryknoll, N.Y.: Orbis Books; London: SCM, 1987) and *Jesus Christ Liberator* by Leonardo Boff (Maryknoll, N.Y.: Orbis Books; London: SPCK, 1978). The latter is fairly technical in parts. Simpler to follow, but more difficult to find (except in India), is *Christ the*

Liberator by John Desrochers (Bangalore: Bangalore Center for Social Action, 1977).

An excellent account of the biblical and historical background for the contemporary reflection is *Jesus, Redeemer and Divine Word* by Gerard S. Sloyan (Wilmington, Del.: Michael Glazier, Inc., 1989).

CHAPTER EIGHT

What Is the Christian Vocation in the World?

If the assertions of the foregoing chapters are true, some far-reaching consequences follow for our understanding of the Christian vocation in the world. The understanding that we inherited from modern but pre–Vatican II times tends to be one of keeping the commandments of God and the Church, participating in the sacramental life of the Church on a regular basis, and staying out of trouble by avoiding occasions of sin and fulfilling the obligations of our state in life. Although not a totally passive description, this account certainly does not encourage initiative, critical evaluation or readiness to adapt to new situations. In fact, it assumes a very static pattern of society and a rather protected position within it. At one time it led to a reluctance on the part of Catholics to engage in politics because of the ambivalent situations in which one might be placed. It also led to attempts to keep young people within church circles lest they be confused or led astray by mixing with others.

Immediately after the Second Vatican Council, some urgent issues arose. In connection with the question about various means of birth control, a more radical question arose: namely, by what criteria can a new issue be resolved for Catholic believers? At that time there was much debate because several successive popes had claimed to give definitive interpretations of the natural law. What gave rise to the debate is that the traditional concept of natural law (as used by the medieval scholastics and subsequently maintained in the Church) seemed to make a definitive interpretation by papal authority impossible. Natural law was held to be the moral order which God has built into the very fabric of creation and which can be discovered by human reason when it is not clouded by self-seeking distortions. The best guarantee of reading the natural law correctly on any issue, therefore, would seem to be the large-scale agreement of well-informed people seeking the truth sincerely and, if at all possible, not having an immediate personal interest in the answer. The papal pronouncements on methods of birth control went against very strong consensus among ethicists of many backgrounds and persuasions who seemed to have a relatively detached view. This in turn raised the question whether perhaps the popes were really claiming to have this teaching from the tradition of Christian faith, but the post-conciliar commissions that were set up to study the matter concluded that such teaching could not be traced to apostolic sources and could not be shown to have a long mainstream history in the Church.

Quite apart from the resolving of the specific issue which had raised the debate, this discussion led to some wider consideration of the morality that is properly Christian. With the help of a number of New Testament scholars, such as Rudolf Schnackenburg, in his book *The Moral Teaching of the New Testament* (English edition issued New York: Herder & Herder, 1965), it became evident that the New Testament gives us, not a code of behavior, but a vision and an inspiration which requires more personal discernment and creativity from the believer. Such preaching of Jesus as the Gospels report contains exhortations of an ideal and visionary nature, such as those in the Sermon on the Mount; or specific advice given to individual people, such as that to the rich young man to sell all his possessions; or exemplary stories that each listener must interpret personally; or such broad and sweeping statements as the proclamation of the great commandment to love God above everything and love one's neighbor as one in destiny with oneself.

This would suggest that what Jesus taught was in no way a new code of behavior; and when asked, he maintained that he had not come to destroy the law but to fulfill it. Nothing in the teaching or behavior of Jesus suggested licentiousness. He assumed the basic morality that we later designated the natural law. He relativized ritual obligations to the more basic human needs of compassion and community. And he called his followers to do more than obey specific commandments. That this was not exactly new in Israel is shown from the answers given him by the lawyer who questioned him about the way to be saved and the greatest commandment. What Scripture scholars tell us is new is the simplicity and the urgency with which Jesus proposed the twofold great commandment as befitting the immediacy of the coming reign of God.

In the aftermath of Vatican II it was realized how far Catholics had, for the most part, diverged from this thinking. What had been substituted was a morality of certainty and safety — a very precise set of rules and instructions, many manuals and guides for examining one's conscience preparatory to making a sacramental confession, frequent directives from Rome about new issues such as Marxist Communism, cremation of the dead, holy days of obligation, fast and abstinence obligations in wartime conditions, contraception, certain elective surgeries, and so forth. Compared with the instructions that Jesus gave his disciples, there seemed to be very little entrusted to the conscience and discernment and good sense of the individual believer or the local communities.

Out of the documents of Vatican II and their progressive implementation there certainly came a certain restlessness among Catholic believers to take more responsibility for their own decisions and their own lives, and in recent years this has caused anxiety in Rome and also among some segments of the local Catholic communities. On the other hand, there has emerged in many sectors of the Church a much keener appreciation of two aspects of Christian discipleship. One is the fact that we cannot be perfect in God's sight by trying to remain safe but, like the three men in the parable of the talents, are intended to act with generosity and initiative and take risks. The other aspect is that in a changing society new needs arise, and that old prescriptions will not cover them. By the enlightenment and empowerment that Christ gives us we are certainly able to meet these challenges and discern how best to act.

However, perhaps the most important issue of all that has come to light is that the Christian vocation in the world is not one of living an unblemished moral life to ensure one's own salvation or to give good example to others. Much less is it to observe a stricter code and be demonstrably better than other people. The Christian vocation is, not to live a moral life (that is simply assumed as background), but to live a redemptive life. A redemptive life assumes that doing the right thing within the structures and values and expectations of the world as it is, is inadequate because the world is not as it ought to be. And this in turn leads inexorably to the idea that it is not enough for us in some sense to renounce the world by detachment from it, actually or in our values. What is required is an alert, critical attitude leading to vigorous and creative initiatives to change the world in which we live and to bring it under the reign of God.

This, of course, is very clearly spelled out in the documents of the Council itself, though only in general principles. It is basic to the Decree *Apostolicam actuositatem* (On the Apostolate of the Laity). The Pastoral Constitution *Gaudium et spes* (On the Church in the Modern World) is entirely based on the assumption that the Christian vocation in the world is to work together to make radical and structural changes, especially on behalf of those who are left out. It is not surprising, therefore, that since that time courses in moral theology, books by moral theologians and discussions at professional meetings and in journals should be concerning themselves so extensively with large social issues, and that the United States Episcopal Conference, for instance, should have issued so many letters dealing with public rather than private morality: on racism, on nuclear disarmament, on the economy and on the role of women in society. Many Catholics, of course, have said and written that church concern with these issues is out of line because they are issues that involve technical expertise and political judgments, and it would be safer for the Church to concern itself with strictly spiritual matters. From the foregoing, however, it should be evident that from a Christian perspective these are spiritual matters because they involve the way we treat one

another (though on a large scale) and our relationships
with one another cannot be separated from our relationship with God.

What has been happening in the Catholic community and causing great concern to some, therefore, is a
disappearance of the neat lines separating the sacred
from the profane, church concerns from everyday
secular concerns. Americans are perhaps particularly
resistant to this because of the national commitment to
separation of Church and state, although in practice this
turns out to be quite an elusive and tricky separation
admitting of many ambiguities and dilemmas. The
Church has in fact never accepted the principle of
separation of Church and state, though in Vatican II, in
the Declaration *Dignitatis humanae* (On Religious
Liberty), there is an affirmation of a related but different
principle of the right of individuals and communities to
social and civil freedom in religious matters. This does
not mean, however, that there can be or should be no
critique of the policies of the state or the effects of the
economy in creating just and inclusive conditions for all
and in maintaining peace and conditions of human
dignity. In fact, the assumptions built into democratic
societies call for such critique and for active participation by all. On the part of a committed Christian

such participation will rightly be informed by a Christian vision of the goal and meaning of human life and Christian assessment of the possibilities of human society in terms of inclusive community, justice and peace.

What is straightforward in enunciating general principles may turn out to be both complex and open to debate in practical applications to specific issues. In the specific issues many factors play a role, and some economic, medical, statistical, sociological, legal or other expertise may be required. It is this in large part that has opened up such a wide field in the theological discussion of public ethical issues and public values. Besides the continuing stream of social encyclicals and other hierarchic statements, there has therefore been a steady stream of publications on social issues from the Christian perspective. Several *Concilium* volumes, beginning with *Faith and the World of Politics,* edited by J. B. Metz (New York: Paulist Press, 1968), have explored the theoretical connections. Other volumes of *Concilium* have collected essays addressing specific issues, as in *War, Poverty, Freedom: The Christian Response,* edited by Franz Böckle (New York: Paulist Press, 1966). At about the same time, Yves Congar's book *Christians Active in the World* (the second half of his work on the priesthood and the lay state) was published in English (New York: Herder & Herder, 1968), arguing the intrinsic vocation of the baptized to act influentially in the world, not under the direction of the hierarchy or as extension of the mission of the hierarchy, but as Church, as a community of disciples.

The resources and authority for this close relationship between theological principles and social action is found both in Scripture and in the traditions of the Church as testified by key texts from various periods of history. *The Faith That Does Justice,* edited by Jesuit theologian John C. Haughey (New York: Paulist Press, 1977), collects the evidence for this in a series of essays analyzing the issues and documenting the ways they were dealt with under changing circumstances from the beginning of the Church to the present. It is noteworthy that this never happened without struggle and that there were always protests from those whose interests were challenged. Yet the strand of continuity is there and is strong, challenging existing assumptions and structures and calling for social change on behalf of suffering or excluded groups. A follow-up volume, *Above Every Name: The Lordship of Christ and Social Systems,* edited by Thomas E. Clarke, a Jesuit theologian on the same research team at Woodstock Theological Center

(New York: Paulist Press, 1980), explores the links between various ways of interpreting the person and mission of Jesus and the attitudes to the Christian vocation in the world. A further volume in the series, *Tracing the Spirit: Communities, Social Action and Theological Reflection,* edited by James E. Hug, also a Woodstock team Jesuit (New York: Paulist Press, 1983), explores the kinds of groups and the kinds of spirituality which lead effectively to strong Christian action in public life.

What emerges from this series (which has been selected here from a wealth of such literature) is, in the first place, the great gap between the vision projected at Vatican II and the spirituality and expectations of most Catholics. Secondly, it is clear that the way we formulate our beliefs has a direct impact on the way we see our vocation in the world, and there continues to be a resistance in the community to giving up certain claims to black-and-white clarity on issues which in practice are very obscure and difficult to resolve. But the emerging theological issue is the tension between the unity of the Church and its hierarchic leadership on the one hand and, on the other, the urgent theologically grounded need for a prophetic and active laity at work in the world and committed to changing structures that

oppress or polarize people. It can be seen quite clearly
that on some key issues like the fate of refugees, the
need for public restraint of profit-motivated policies of
large and powerful companies, the need for redeploy-
ment of the resources in the armaments industry, and so
forth, hierarchic authorities are often far ahead of the
community of church members. In these matters theological scholarship and church hierarchic utterances tend
to be closely linked, but where practical economic and
political interest and privileges are threatened, the resistance of more traditional Catholics is strong and finds
its justification in the thesis that these are not matters of
faith or Catholic observance.

It is one of the concerns of current Catholic theology dealing with public issues of peace, justice and
community, to break into the cycle that makes it possible for these attitudes to persist. This is a cycle of faith
formulation assigning boundaries to what may be
demanded by church authority, by the very definition of
what is a matter of faith or religious concern. Deep
respect and unquestioning obedience are professed, but
are operative only within the realm traditionally seen as
religious, even when both scholarly exposition and
hierarchical exhortation demonstrate the larger implica-

tions of the gospel of Jesus Christ and the redemption of the world that is still incomplete.

Besides the issues in which the principles are clear but there is resistance against the practical implications, there are, of course, many issues in which it is very difficult to identify even appropriate principles. These include numerous issues in the biomedical sphere which constitute tragic dilemmas either because of the scarcity of resources for very costly life-saving procedures, or because there is no way of doing what is best for everyone in the situation, or because it is not possible to know the outcomes and calculate the risks. There are many such issues in which wrestling with the Christian vocation in the world gives no certitude that one knows exactly what is right, but instead involves risk, sensitivity and the balancing of incompatible values. This kind of struggle with moral decision making and efforts to act redemptively in bad situations is perhaps a more normal experience of the Christian vocation in a world still needing to be redeemed than the comfortable certainty of obeying well-defined laws in predictable situations.

Suggestions for Further Reading

Christians Active in the World by Yves Congar (New York: Herder & Herder; London: Burns & Oates, 1968) can be recommended as a starting point in pursuing the understanding of the Christian vocation. *The Faith That Does Justice,* edited by John C. Haughey (New York: Paulist Press, 1977), explores various particular aspects of redemptive Christian presence in the world.

Besides the various volumes mentioned in this chapter, there is a comprehensive collection of essays which might be recommended: *One Hundred Years of Catholic Social Thought,* edited by John Coleman (Maryknoll, N.Y.: Orbis Books, 1991).

CHAPTER NINE

Is There Convergence of Goals and Values Among the Religions?

As theological reflection on Christian faith, hope and practice has come to terms with the complexities of the modern world, one of the consequences has been a gradual engagement in ecumenism not only among Christians but also in the wider realm of the great world religions, including those with no historical connection to the Hebrew Scriptures. We seem to be swept into an irreversible trend of the mingling of cultures and peoples in pluralistic societies, in which we can no longer ignore one another's beliefs and religious commitments. The questions that arise tend towards a certain degree of secularization. Secularization, not secularism, is the tendency to formulate beliefs and traditions in the language of common experience and to try to grasp the meaning of faith commitments in terms of the difference they make in everyday behavior and expectations.

This kind of trend inevitably leads to questions like whether we are worshipping the same God under different names, what constitutes idolatry and what is simply a different approach to the sacred, whether our hopes for the human situation converge, whether our aims for peace and justice admit of cooperation across religious boundaries, whether we share the same sense of right and wrong, and so forth. These questions are no longer a matter for mere curiosity or speculation but have become immediately and intensely practical.

Earlier discussion in this field revolved mainly around the question whether there is salvation in the other religions. We have established the answer to this: those who follow other religions can certainly be saved, and that not in spite of but through those religions. This does not mean that all religions are equally good. Traditions that demand human sacrifice or practice physical cruelty of various kinds are, by Christian standards, misled and misleading. But this would be equally true of some interpretations of Christianity in the past as it would be of other traditions. Traditions that focus on ritual to the point of neglecting human need and suffering are, by Christian standards, less salvific. And this also would be true of some interpretations of Christianity as well as of some other religious traditions. This being said, however, what was once thought of as a rather questionable position put forth by authors like Heinz Schlette in *Towards a Theology of Religions* (New York: Herder & Herder, 1966) and Eugene Hillman in *The Wider Ecumenism: Anonymous Christianity and the Church* (New York: Herder & Herder, 1968) is now very generally accepted. This is due, at least in part, to Vatican II's *Nostra aetate* (On the Relation of the Church to Non-Christian Religions) and to the encyclical of Pope Paul VI *Ecclesiam suam* (His Church). These documents certainly put a stamp of official approval on a more open-minded approach to other religious traditions.

The advances in the wider ecumenism are also due, no doubt, to the increasing opportunities for sustained discussion and study of one another's traditions. Many initiatives in this direction have broadened the discussion so that it is no longer a matter for a few specialists but one that must be addressed in most of the work in systematic theology today. The two areas in which this has become most evident are Christology and the theology of revelation. Few new books in Christology published now are able to avoid the question whether Jesus is properly named the only savior, and in what ways Jesus is to be compared and contrasted with other great religious figures in the world, such as Buddha and Mohammed. In his book *Jesus Christ and the Encounter of Religions* (Maryknoll, N.Y.: Orbis Books, 1991), Jacques Dupuis, a French Jesuit teaching at the Gregorian University in Rome and formerly involved in the World Council of Churches and the Pontifical (Catholic) Council for Inter-religious Dialogue, considers the question of Jesus in relation to Hinduism in particular and non-Christian religions in general. He finds that the irreducible particularity of Jesus in the Christian faith is part of a larger difference with Hinduism which has to do with the significance of history. Yet he acknowledges both that Hinduism has a wisdom to offer to Christians and that it presents some important challenges to our formulations of Christology.

A more radical position concerning the place of Jesus in relation to other religions has been proposed by Paul Knitter, among others, in his book *No Other Name? A Critical Study of Christian Attitudes Towards the World Religions* (Maryknoll, N.Y.: Orbis Books, 1985), and in a volume edited jointly with John Hick, *The Myth of Christian Uniqueness* (Maryknoll, N.Y.: Orbis Books, 1987). These authors make a claim for what they call a pluralistic stance which seems to involve the renunciation of claims to finality, definitive or absolute truth or universality. They find that other Christian authors writing on the relations among the religions are either inconclusive or unduly patronizing in their statements on the relationship between Christianity and the world religions. The pluralist position in turn, however, was taken to task in the volume *Christian Uniqueness Reconsidered,* edited by Gavin D'Costa (Maryknoll, N.Y.: Orbis Books, 1990). The role of Jesus, though not the only issue, was central in these reflections. Perhaps the most that can be said at this stage of the discussion is that, while sure that salvation in Christ is potentially universal, we do not know ultimate truth and do not know other faith traditions from the inside, but we do know that they are worthy of respect and that we can learn from them, while engaged in a friendly wager concerning the centrality we see for Jesus in history.

The question of revelation is the more central one in Raimundo Panikkar's *The Silence of God: The Answer of the Buddha* (Maryknoll, N.Y.: Orbis Books, 1990), which, as the title implies, deals with issues that inevitably arise in Christian-Buddhist dialogue because the ultimate is understood as non-personal in Buddhism. Panikkar, an internationally renowned Catholic scholar of world religions with roots in both Hindu and Spanish culture, is able to show corresponding strands in Christian tradition that make this Buddhist approach more comprehensible as another religious path with serious claims. Christians have, in fact, much to learn from Buddhism concerning spirituality and the intellectual humility that is the foundation for any real religious faith.

The bases and boundaries for the wider ecumenism are very thoroughly explored in the collection *Christianity and the Wider Ecumenism*, edited by Peter Phan (New York: Paragon House Publications, 1990). Under the editorship of Peter Phan, professor of theology at the Catholic University of America, what these essays show, even in the diversity of the positions they take, is the degree to which the concerns of the world religions do converge on many issues of practical importance for our world — issues of peace, world justice, and so forth — and the degree to which Christian theologians are coming to realize and acknowledge this. Most of the authors in this volume (who are all Christians) acknowledge important debts to representatives of other religious traditions with whom they have been in dialogue and sometimes in working partnership.

What might be said, then, about the convergence of religions, is that they have their own traditions, symbol systems, rituals of worship and ways of life. It is quite possible that continuing cultural exchanges and secularization will tend to soften the difference and particularity, but that this is not likely to be any great gain. We need the particular in which we feel at home and in which the symbols convey more than can be spelled out in secular and common language. We need the particular of other people's traditions because our own is often understood better in the comparison and juxtaposition. Moreover, we need the particular of the other traditions because no language or symbol system can capture the whole of reality and the whole of human experience in all historical strands.

Yet there is an area of convergence which is important and which should certainly be fostered. It embraces mutual respect and tolerance, inter-faith community harmony and personal inter-faith friendships. It also embraces a sincere desire to know more about one another's traditions and to disseminate that knowledge in order to dispel prejudice and suspicion. Most of all, it should involve constant efforts to collaborate for peace on a world-wide basis and on all levels of society, and constant explorations for possible ways to collaborate in meeting urgent human needs for food, shelter, human living conditions, inclusion in social and political life, health care and access to education.

It may be that because Christianity has passed through the challenges and transformations of the Enlightenment, Christians have a special role of mediation between some of the other traditions in which exchange and collaboration on common endeavors may be more difficult to achieve. And this may be not only an opportunity but, in some sense, an obligation, because the colonialism practiced by Christian nations has brought about many of the rivalries and territorial disputes that divide peoples of different religious traditions in the contemporary world. From a Catholic perspective, the possibilities for this have greatly increased in the last several decades because of the ever more confident approach to the wider ecumenism.

Suggestions for Further Reading

There is a great deal of literature from the last several decades on relations among the religions, comparison of their teachings and interpretations, and Christian theological accounts of the other religions. Of these, those that offer a comparative description and analysis are probably the easiest to understand and the best to begin with. Two such are *Jesus Christ at the Encounter of World Religions* by Jacques Dupuis (Maryknoll, N.Y.: Orbis Books, 1991), using Christian-Hindu encounter as the example, and *The Silence of God* by Raimundo Panikkar (Maryknoll, N.Y.: Orbis Books, 1989), using Buddhism as the example.

Two interesting and helpful books on specific topics as treated by different traditions are: *For the Sake of the World* by Patrick Henry and Donald Swearer (Minneapolis: Augsburg Fortress, 1988), comparing Buddhist and Christian monasticism; and *Concilium* (unnumbered): *The Ethics of World Religions and Human Rights,* edited by Hans Küng and Jürgen Moltmann (Philadelphia: Trinity Press International; London: SCM, 1990). I have tried to do something similar in my book *A Case for Peace in Reason and Faith* (Collegeville, Minn.: The Liturgical Press, 1992), drawing on peace teachings of various traditions.

For Christian theology about other religions, three books might especially be recommended. The first of these is *Many Paths* by Eugene Hillman (Maryknoll, N.Y.: Orbis Books, 1989), which argues the theological consequences of the opening to other religions in the Second Vatican Council. It requires close attention but is worth the effort. A second is *Christianity and the Wider Ecumenism,* edited by Peter Phan (New York: Paragon House Publications, 1990), containing essays from Catholic and from various Protestant perspectives on the theological issues involved in relations with communities of the other religions. The third book that offers a special perspective is *Christian Uniqueness Reconsidered* edited by Gavin D'Costa (Maryknoll, N.Y.: Orbis Books, 1990), which contains essays on Christian identity and faith in the light of the world religions.

CHAPTER TEN

Is Trinitarian Faith Still Relevant?

One of the entirely unexpected results of the post–Vatican II quest to answer the urgent practical questions for contemporary believers is a new interest in trinitarian theology. It is an unexpected result simply because all the aforementioned questions arise out of people's attempts to deal with current developments in the Church and in the world. The reflection on the trinitarian faith of Christians is not that kind of question. Yet recent theological writings and conferences have been concerned with this as an issue that cannot be set aside any longer if the whole fabric of the faith is to hold together in a way that contemporary believers can grasp.

Christian faith from the very beginning has been insistent that the God of our faith is the one transcendent God of Israel, the creator of all that is, both material and spiritual, and the one who holds all things in existence and all creation in balance towards a unifying goal. But side by side with this has been the claim that we have met the One God in human history quite concretely in Jesus of Nazareth, and that now as always, the divine is not only transcendent and at the same time objectively present in history, but is also simultaneously within believers and within their community, enhancing their being and empowering them to transcend their limitations and their isolation.

This understanding is enshrined in our traditional creeds, expressed in the sign of the cross and the doxologies, and developed as the framework of the faith in theology and catechesis. Yet the common experience of believers is that they assent to this notionally but can see no practical impact on their lives. If they become aware of the trinitarian character of the Christian understanding of God, it is usually because they discover in their own prayer some confusion over whether they are addressing Jesus or the Father, and whether this matters, and whether they are supposed to think of the Holy Spirit in personal or impersonal terms. Most people manage somehow to resolve this type of question, and then return to their former habit of ignoring the trinitarian claims or enshrining them in a sacred mental space of irrelevance.

Theologians, however, have had to address the question of what we really mean when we pray to and speak of God as triune. They have had to address the question because, pressed by ordinary believers to deal with questions of experience in a way that will be intelligible in terms of our contemporary ways of experiencing and interpreting reality, they have been obliged to consider again how all aspects of our faith form an integrated worldview. When they do this, they keep finding that what has held the whole system of beliefs, hopes and commitments together over the Christian centuries is the revelation of the triune God, and the relating of all aspects of Christian life and worship to that revelation. With this realization, the theologians have been compelled to go back to the sources in Scripture and the early Church — back to the story line in the way that the early Christians gave an account of their situation in history and of their hopes for themselves and for the world. Out of this quest have come several common themes to be found in authors of the last decade or so.

The first of these common themes is that it is not out of speculation but out of Christian spirituality that the doctrine of the Trinity emerges and becomes the central pivot of the faith. The second common theme is the realization that trinitarian ways of thinking about God correspond to the insight that it is not self-determination as isolated individuals but the capacity for relationship and community that is most central in our own human personhood and identity. This has been part of a self-critical evaluation of our intensely individualistic contemporary Western industrialized culture. We do not see God directly but as reflected in ourselves as creatures of God, so our concepts of God tend to be fashioned in our own image as we perceive that image. In the post-Enlightenment era of rational individualism it is not surprising that the emphasis has been on the eternal, perfect and unchangeable oneness of God, creator but withdrawn in splendid isolation. The inadequacy and corruption of the social fabric heralded by such individualistic thinking and attitudes have prompted a reassessment of the essence of the human as it reflects the reality of the divine.

A third common theme is the admission that we cannot, by the nature of the case, have direct access to the intrinsic nature or being of God, as though God were an object that could be observed and studied. What we can know is something of God's dealings with us, as observed from our end of the relationship. That means that in the final analysis discourse about the divine Trinity is really discourse about salvation history, about the way we are being drawn into a more intimate and fulfilling relationship with God. Therefore speculative theology about the trinity of God never gets beyond the elaboration of analogies taken from our own lives. No matter how abstract, esoteric or philosophical the language of such discussion, it cannot make the qualitative leap into knowledge of the intrinsic being of God. This is very important because it implies that new and creative ways of speaking and writing about the relationships between Father, Word (Son) and Spirit are legitimate, and ought to be intelligible as analogies.

A fourth common theme in the contemporary writers on trinitarian theology is the understanding that we do not first come to know God as absolute being and then extrapolate to the idea that God is love. It is rather the other way around. We first come to know God as love — that is, as gracious self-communication — and then extrapolate to the idea that God is ground of all being. This makes an important difference also, because it is founded in human experience — parental and family experience, historical experience, community building experience. In other words, such grounding removes trinitarian theology from the realm of an intellectual game played by a few rather untypical human individuals, to the realm of practical discernment of what is ultimately worthwhile and imperative in human lives.

A masterly work dealing with such efforts to engage in trinitarian theology responsibly and wisely is that of Dominican theologian William J. Hill, of the Catholic University of America, *The Three Personed God* (Washington: Catholic University of America Press, 1982). Tracing the Hebrew sense of "Word of God" and "Breath (Spirit) of God" through the variety of symbols for differentiation in God, Hill considers what patristic, medieval and modern authors have made of this symbolism, coming to it with their own prior expectations and their own characteristic sense of what is real. He shows that modern authors have retraveled some of the historical routes of debate and have come back to the historical and communal dimensions of human experience of divine salvation, and to the acknowledgement of mystery. Two aspects of his survey are astonishing: first, the number of theologians dealing with trinitarian theology, of whom he discusses nineteen from the the twentieth century, many still living and writing; and secondly, the convergence of these authors towards taking the historical as the basis, and focusing on relationship, love and community as the human experiences on which analogies for the divine must be built. The practical implications of this have been spelled out at some length by several contemporary authors.

Among those working out such a contemporary approach is the Australian Redemptorist theologian Anthony Kelly in *The Trinity of Love* (Wilmington, Del.: Michael Glazier, Inc., 1989). He begins with the point that the Christian Church has been constituted by trinitarian faith in its life and its worship. The Church experienced itself as people of God fathered by Jesus in the Spirit, and said so constantly, and prayed accordingly. This is as true today as it was in the beginning of Christianity, so that Kelly proposes the living, worshipping community as the starting point for understanding the doctrine of the Trinity. This leads him to take the experiential foundations and the creative, constitutive power of love relationship seriously as models for personal, community and political becoming in the world. A similar theme emerges in *God for Us: The Trinity and Christian Life* by Catherine Mowry La-Cugna, lay theologian at the University of Notre Dame (San Francisco: HarperCollins, 1992). Making a detailed study of certain Church Fathers and medieval theologians, she shows from history the conditions under which trinitarian faith was alive and shaping Christian conceptions of community, and other conditions under which it stagnated, became abstract and irrelevant to practical life. Her truly important contribution is the link she makes between the emergence of orthodox trinitarian faith and genuine community. The rejection of "subordinationist" concepts of the Trinity (those which made Word and Spirit less than fully divine) is related to a radically new way of building human community based on free participation of all and not on patterns of domination.

A vigorous statement along similar lines was made by Brazilian theologian Leonardo Boff in *Trinity and Society* (Maryknoll, N.Y.: Orbis Books, 1988). Boff sees the true doctrine of the Trinity as a liberating one. It implies that the fundamental reality which should shape our attitudes and expectations is that of community or communion. Moreover, that fundamental reality is one of complementarity of uniqueness without patterns of subordination or domination. Boff traces the history of the trinitarian doctrine in more detail than any of the other authors mentioned here. He also offers very pertinent reflections on the way the symbolism can be used and has been used, and the impact such uses can have on the structures and values of a Christian society. Like Mowry LaCugna, he proposes a way of seeing and expressing the symbolism that will be liberating rather than oppressive, but he does so with a great deal of highly technical language.

An overview of what has been written suggests that what has freed so much new creativity in the field has been the insistence of Karl Rahner and Piet Schoonenberg, many decades ago, that the word *person* used about God is not only analogous rather than the same as that word used about ourselves. It is not even the same but analogous when used about Father, Son and Spirit. What this means is that the expression "three persons in one God" may be giving people a false idea of the doctrine in our times, because it is not understood as it would have been in the fourth and fifth centuries by speakers of Latin and Greek who were in a position to take an interest in the formulation of the doctrine. This point made by Rahner and Schoonenberg has served, among other things, to alert theologians to the fact that Scripture and early church tradition offered a variety of ways of speaking about the triune God. The Bible offers the imagery (in Genesis and again in John's Prologue) of God's speaking, which shapes things, and God's breathing, which gives them life. In the beginning "God said," and it happened; things came to order, so to speak. And "the Spirit hovered" over the waters, and life emerged from them; God "breathed into" what had been fashioned from clay, and it became a living human being. In Irenaeus of Lyons — a Church Father of the late second century in southern Gaul in a Greek-speaking community — there is another way of imaging this. Irenaeus speaks of Word and Spirit as the two hands of God, creating and guiding through history to salvation, one hand shaping human beings to the likeness of the divine in an external way, and the other hand shaping them to the divine image inwardly.

Scripture and tradition also give us imagery of Law and Wisdom as partners of the creator, and of the light and its radiance, the original and the reflection or icon. There are many non-personal analogies which may speak to us today much more eloquently of a divine reality which encompasses us in every aspect of our

being, while we can never encompass it whether intel-
lectually or in any other way. Our trinitarian faith
expresses this testimony of our experience in history
and in the community of the faithful, and expresses it in
paradoxes for which we do not apologize precisely
because we try to give utterance to a mystery which is
larger than the power of our language. But it is a mystery whose exigence carries into all phases of our life in
the world.

Suggestions for Further Reading

None of the books mentioned is easy reading for the non-specialist. Some may actually find it best to begin with *The Trinitarian Controversy* by William G. Rusch (Fortress, 1980), which is an anthology of the texts from the early centuries in which the standard trinitarian doctrine was established.

The volume *Trinity and Society* by Leonardo Boff (Maryknoll, N.Y.: Orbis Books, 1988) explains itself as it goes along but needs very close attention. A volume that may also be accessible to the non-specialist is that of Bruno Forte, *The Trinity as History* (New York: Alba House, 1989), which is simply descriptive or narrative in parts, but abstract in other parts, and in a few sections quotes a good deal in Latin. Some readers may react negatively to a certain "churchiness" of style.

Very demanding of concentration and close study are the other three books which were mentioned in the chapter: William J. Hill, *The Three Personed God* (Washington: Catholic University of America Press,

1982); Catherine Mowry LaCugna, *God for Us* (San Francisco: HarperCollins, 1991); and Anthony Kelly, *The Trinity of Love* (Wilmington, Del.: Michael Glazier, Inc., 1989).

INDEX